CELESTIAL SYMBOLS

Symbolism in Doctrine, Religious Traditions and Temple Architecture

Allen H. Barber

ISBN: 0-88290-344-6
Horizon Publishers' Catalog and Order Number: 1025
First Printing, March, 1989

Second Printing,
Revised Edition: May, 1990

Printed and distributed
in the United States of America by

Horizon
Publishers
& Distributors, Incorporated
P.O. Box 490 Bountiful, Utah 84011-0490

TABLE OF CONTENTS

PART ONE
THE PURPOSE AND NATURE OF SYMBOLS

1. Religious Symbolism **11**

The Symbols In The Plan of Salvation 11
What a Symbol Is 11
The Ancient Use of Symbols 12
Discerning True Symbols 13
The Arrangement of Symbols in This Book 13

2. Miscellaneous Secular and Religious Symbols **15**

Recognizing and Understanding Symbols 15
Many Symbols Point to Jesus Christ 16
The Lord's Guiding Hand 19
Numbers Used as Symbols 22
The All-Seeing Eye 24

3. Miscellaneous Geometric Symbols **26**

The LDS Church's Claim on Symbols 26
Geometrical Symbols 26
The Cross, Circle and Square 27
The Stars as Symbols 30
Triangles and Their Variations 31
The Interlaced Triangle or Star of David 34
Abbreviations and Combination of Symbols 35

PART TWO
CELESTIAL POSSIBILITIES

4. The Eternal Nature of the Universe **41**

The Importance of Knowledge Concerning the Universe 41
An Infinite Universe 41

Priesthood the Governing Power 43
The Nature of the Godhead and Mankind 44
The Purpose of God's Creations 45
Degrees in God's Realm 46
Who and What is God 48
The Celestial Family Chain 49
A Tangible Kingdom of Activity 50

5. The Earth's Creation and the Garden of Eden 52

Spirits Chosen to Inhabit the Earth 50
The Creation of the Earth and Those Who Dwell Thereon 55
Adam and Eve in the Garden of Eden .55
Satan's Temptation of Eve 57
The Symbolic Counterparts Between
   the Garden and Mortality 58
Adam and Eve Chastized and the Earth Cursed 59
Adam and Eve Cast Out of Eden 60
Satan's Influence Continues 62

6. Pointing Towards Christ's Atonement 63

Christ Chosen as Savior 63
Adam and Eve Begin Mortal Life 63
Sacrifices as Symbols of Christ and His Life 64
Symbolic Sacrifices Many and Varied 66
The Serpent Also a Symbol of Christ 67
Christ and His Atoning Sacrifice 68

PART THREE
MAN'S LIFESPAN BETWEEN BIRTH AND RESURRECTION

7. Probation in the Physical World 71

The Plan of Salvation 71
Man Can Become as God 72
The Priesthood on Earth and in Heaven 74
The Sustaining of Proper Authority 76

8. The First Principles and Ordinances of the Gospel.......**78**

Faith and Repentance 78
Baptism as the Gateway 79
Baptism as a Complex Symbol.......................... 79
Baptism into the Family of Christ 82
Baptism by Fire and the Holy Ghost.................... 83
Baptism of the Earth.................................. 85

9. The Lord's Commandments **87**

The Sacrament as a Renewal of the Baptismal Covenants 87
Anointing and Administrations 90
The Symbolism of God's Commandments 90
Adversity and Service Develops Talents 92
The Importance of a Healthy Mind and Body 94
Tithing and Service to Others 95

10. The Family Sealed for Time and Eternity.............**99**

The Patriarchal Order of the Priesthood 99
The Proper Marriage and Sealing 100
The Relationship Between Husband and Wife.............. 102
Ordinances Must Be Sealed for Validity 103

11. Life in the Spirit World **105**

Spirit Life is Much the Same as Earth Life 105
The State of the Wicked 106
The State of the Righteous 108
The Intermediate State of Spirits 108
Everyone to Hear the Gospel 110

12. Symbols Related to the Millennium
    and Resurrection **115**

The Earth to Return to a Paradisiacal Glory 115
Baptism of the Earth by Fire........................... 116
The Signs of Christ's Second Coming 118
The Death and Resurrection of the Earth................. 118
The Resurrection of Mankind........................... 120

The Differences of Bodies and Degrees in the Resurrection . . . 122
The Righteous to Reside as Eternal
     Parents With Heavenly Father 123

PART FOUR
THE HOUSE OF THE LORD

13. Ceremonies and Ordinances of the Temples **126**

The Temple as a Symbolic Beacon Toward Eternal Life 126
The Temple Ordinances and Ceremonies 129
Sealing by Proxy 131
The Temple Endowment 132
The Modes and Methods of Endowment Instruction 134
The Principles and Ordinances of the Temple 137

14. Symbols and Revelation in and on the Temple **140**

The Physical Symbols on the Salt Lake City Temple 140
Wall Buttresses Containing the
     Earth, Moon and Sun Stones 141
The Miscellaneous Physical Symbols
     on the Salt Lake Temple 145
The Symbols on the East and West Doors 148
The Temples as Places for Revelation 155
Spiritual Experiences Available in the Temple 158

15. Expanding Horizons **162**

Alpha and Omega on LDS Buildings 163
The Manti Temple Door Hardware 165
Symbolic Flowers, Rosettes, and Designs in Temples 168
Popular Use of Flowers, Rosettes and Other Designs 170

Bibliography and Indexes **178**

ACKNOWLEDGMENT AND DEDICATION

Gathering, writing, and rewriting the material for this book has taken several years and considerable time. I wish to acknowledge my appreciation to my wife Nora W. Barber for the many hours she has spent helping me and the many inconveniences she has endured. She has not only offered suggestions and typed and retyped parts or all of the manuscript many times, but has helped with the verification of sources. Also to Duane S. Crowther, President and Editor of Horizon Publishers, who gave me considerable advice, direction and encouragement in rewriting portions of the manuscript in preparation for the publication of this book.

I want to dedicate this book to my wife, my children, and all of my posterity, for I realize, as the message in this book proclaims, the greatest reward of all is to reside with our family in the Celestial Kingdom of God. May all of you discover for yourselves that this is true.

Allen H. Barber

Chapter One

RELIGIOUS SYMBOLISM

The Symbols In The Plan of Salvation

Symbolism has been a fascinating subject for almost everyone for many centuries. The study of symbolism has been approached from many angles and for many reasons. The purpose of this book is to identify and explain religious symbols which relate to God's plan of salvation, for the gospel of Christ is the basic foundation for all true symbolism. The book will show how God uses symbols to teach mankind the plan of life and salvation from the time of the creation, through earthlife, and into immortality.

What a Symbol Is

A symbol, according to Webster's Dictionary, is "a sign by which one knows or infers a thing; that which suggests something else by reason of relationship, association, etc." Funk and Wagnalls Company dictionary states: "Symbolism...stretches the capacity of both expression and comprehension and becomes the medium through which some of the most universal, elemental and intangible concepts of man are conveyed."

As an example of how symbols are used, wedding rings are exchanged at a marriage ceremony as a symbol of the marriage union. Since the ring has no end, it represents a love that is expected to last unceasingly throughout mortal life. (*Signs and Sym.*, p. 318) But neither does a ring have a beginning, and with no beginning nor ending the ring becomes a symbol of an eternity of life to members of The Church of Jesus Christ of Latter-day Saints. The Prophet Joseph Smith said: "I take my ring from my finger and liken it unto the mind of man, the immortal part, because it has no beginning. Suppose you cut it in two; then it has a beginning and an end; but join it again and it continues one eternal round. So with the spirit of man." (*Teachings*, p. 354)

The Ancient Use of Symbols

In order to recognize and understand the extent and reasons why symbolism is used, one must realize that there is a Supreme Being with power that controls the universe. He has used and still uses symbols to teach mankind the true principles and laws of the universe as pertaining to His eternal plan of life and salvation.

Many objects and ideas are used as symbols. The sun, moon, stars, trees, wind and love are some of the most common. Words, letters and pictures are symbols of that which they represent. Flags and national anthems represent their country. The parables that Christ taught are a type of symbol.

Until the past few centuries there was not an abundance of writing to convey messages so symbols were an important part of communication. In the era of Adam and the early prophets, symbols were used extensively to teach gospel principles. As certain ideas were taught in detail, symbols were used to associate with and emphasize a particular concept. Then, as the symbol was subsequently used, it brought the idea or message to the mind of the beholder. Frederick R. Webber states, "From the very beginning God Almighty used symbolism to teach important truths." (*Church*, p. 25)

Many people read the Bible or other scriptures but do not understand nor enjoy the symbolic or deeper meanings in the material they're reading. They think and interpret what they are reading only in terms of their personal background and culture. To understand a symbol, the reader must think about the imagery on the basis of by whom and for whom the symbol was given and how the interpretation fits in God's overall plan of life and salvation.

Although symbolic teachings given to Adam and the ancient prophets were correct and true, some of them have become distorted as they have filtered down through many different channels. Other symbols have originated from the ideas of men based on particular customs and traditions of the time. James Churchward claims that the wide scope of many symbols and their similar meanings prove them to have originated from the same source. (*Lost Continent*, p. 135)

Discerning True Symbols

Some of the symbols in this book are referred to or quoted from books written by those whose material may or may not represent true and correct symbols of God's teachings. However, one can gain a greater understanding of how true gospel principles were taught by ancient prophets by examining many different symbols. One can accept the symbols found in the scriptures, those set forth by the prophets, and those revealed in a temple of the Lord as true representations of the gospel plan of life and salvation, but he should analyze others carefully to determine their truthfulness. Such sources are the best guidelines for any symbolic representations quoted from this book. The scriptures and the Lord's temple ceremonies are full of symbolic representations which are intended to be understood by those who diligently and prayerfully study them. The Lord said, "I have also spoken by the prophets, and I have multiplied visions, and used similitudes, by the ministry of the prophets." (Hosea 12:10) In a few instances where I have not had a source for a particular idea, the symbol presented is of my own personal opinion and should be considered as such.

Words such as *similitude, resemblance, counterpart, likeness, type, significance, represent,* usually denote a symbolic representation. These words will be italicized so that the reader may more easily recognize the words intended as symbols. Names of books may also be italicized.

The Arrangement of Symbols in This Book

This book will first describe a miscellaneous number of geometric, architectural and gospel symbols that refer to general concepts and religious teachings of the gospel. The balance of the book deals with symbols as they are directly relate to God's plan of life and salvation. The scope of His plan encompasses the universe, His position therein, the power by which He governs it, and the great potential mankind has to become exalted with Him.

The chapters begin by describing many miscellaneous symbols. Next they describe the nature of God's domain in the universe. Celestial glory in this domain is mankind's highest goal of achievement. Symbols explain the birth of God's spirit children in pre-earth life and the creation of an earth for these spirits to experience mortal life. Adam and Eve, the first of these spirits, are placed in the Garden of Eden. A narrative relates their experience in the Garden and after being cast out, which symbolizes mankind's transition from pre-mortal to mortal life. The discussions cover man's mortal birth and his sojourn through mortal life. They depict man's life as a proving experience, with the many symbols God uses to instruct him in the principles and commandments required in order for him to return to Eternal father's realm are explained. The chapters continue with mankind's death, his sojourn in the spirit world, his judgment and resurrection. They explain the millennium, and the death and resurrection of the earth as a celestial globe where the righteous may dwell.

The final chapters explain the manner in which the concepts and principles outlined in this book are taught in the temples of the Lord. In the temples the highest and most spiritual teachings of God's plan of life and salvation are presented in courses of symbolic instruction.

Chapter Two

MISCELLANEOUS SECULAR AND RELIGIOUS SYMBOLS

Recognizing and Understanding Symbols

There are hundreds of symbols in the scriptures, and many others exist in secular writings. Most of the latter are derived from man-made ideas or have become corrupted as they have sifted down as verbal traditions loosely based on the original teachings of the early prophets. Those that more closely conform to the true principles of the gospel have been selected for the readers of this book to use as a guide to more fully understand the purpose and meaning of symbols, and their use in teaching the plan of salvation. In a few cases the author has given his personal interpretation of a particular symbolic representation.

To demonstrate how much better one can understand the Lord's messages in the scriptures if he or she looks beyond the surface meaning let us examine some of the ideas one may consider as *symbolic representation* in the Lord's encounter with Satan. "Jesus was led up of the spirit, into the wilderness...and when He had fasted forty days and forty nights...he was afterwards an hungered, and was left to be tempted of the devil." (Matthew 4:1-10) The term wilderness, in the scriptures, often *denotes* the gentile nations of the world. (Isaiah 34:1 & 35:1; 1 Nephi 1:4; D & C 109:73) *Likewise* Adam was left in the Garden of Eden to be tempted of the devil and then entered into the wilderness of the world wherein mankind is tempted or tried by the devil.

Christ's first temptation or trial was of hunger, "a temptation of appetite." (David O. McKay, *Conference Report*, Oct. 1911, p. 59) The tempter challenged Him to change stones to bread. Jesus gave no reference to satisfying His own bodily hunger; instead He said "Man shall not live by bread alone, but by every word that proceedeth out of the mouth of God." Therefore, Christ's hunger *symbolized* the hunger that man should have for the Gospel of Jesus Christ. Christ *symbolically* is called the bread of life and from Him comes the eternal bread of life and living waters. (John 6:32-35)

For the second temptation Jesus was set "on the pinnacle of the temple" which would *represent* some high place, situation, or condition of mankind. The devil told Jesus to "cast thyself down" and the angels "shall bear thee up, lest at any time thou dash thy foot against a stone." A stone sometimes *represents* the Gospel of Jesus Christ or the Kingdom of God. (Daniel 2:44-45; D & C 65:2) This temptation makes more sense if it means that Christ could fall from His Godship and kick against His Church. *Symbolically* Satan is continually tempting mankind to venture from the safety of the pinnacle of righteousness and "cast" himself or herself down into a life of evil. He tries to assure the tempted that the angels will deliver him from the consequences of breaking the commandments of God or dashing "thy foot against a stone." But Jesus said, "And whosoever shall fall on this stone shall be broken..." (Matthew 21:44) President McKay said the second temptation is "a yielding to the pride and fashion and vanity of those alienated from the things of God." (McKay, *Conference Report*, Oct. 1911, p. 59)

In the third temptation Jesus was taken "up into an exceedingly high mountain and showeth him the kingdoms of the world and the glory of them...And the Devil...said, all these things will I give unto thee if thou wilt fall down and worship me." (Matthew 4:8-9) This third temptation is *symbolically* material in nature and as such is in *similitude* of the "gratifying of the passions or desires for the riches of the world, or power among men." (McKay, *Conference Report*, Oct. 1911, p. 59) Since the worship of power and material things *represents* worship of the devil, if a person wants eternal life, he or she must say as did Jesus, "Get thee hence, Satan, for it is written, Thou shalt worship the Lord thy God, and him only shalt thou serve." (Matthew 4:10)

Many Symbols Point to Jesus Christ

There are several legends among the American Indians in Mexico and Central America that are deeply entrenched in *symbolism*. One of these consists of a "white bearded God" that came to their ancestors centuries ago through the air, then promised as he left, that he would return to them again. The Quetzal bird, being very beautiful, reminded them of the manner in which their heavenly visitor came and left, so they selected this bird as a *symbol* of this Being. (*Archaeology* p. 31; *Christ in America*, pp. 116-124; *Sacred*, p. 196) The *Book of Mormon* records a visit of Jesus Christ after his resurrection to the people on the American continent in which He descended out of heaven *like* a bird, after which he ascended back into heaven. (3 Nephi 11:8; 18:39) From this visit the Quetzal bird became a *symbol* of Christ's visit to America two thousand years ago.

The *symbol* expanded into Quetzacoatl which is a combination of the Quetzal bird and Coatl, an ancient Mexican word for serpent. (*Christ in America*, pp. 116-124; *Sacred Symbols*, pp. 196-197) The serpent has been a *symbol* of Christ since Moses made a serpent of brass and placed in on a pole to *represent* to the Israelites that "as Moses lifted up the serpent in the wilderness even so must the Son of Man be lifted up" on the cross. (John 3:14; Numbers 21:8-9) When Lehi and his family came to America, they brought with them the early records of the Israelites; consequently, when Christ visited their posterity on the American continent, Lehi's descendants knew that the *symbol* of the serpent *represented* Christ. (2 Nephi 25:20) Later generations gradually used this information to form the quetzal-coatl bird-serpent *symbol* which is found carved on the ruins of many buildings and ancient temples in Mexico and Central America depicting traditions of a God who *represented* both a heavenly being and a serpent.

The Quetzal bird is primarily green in color *indicating* new life and growth as Jesus Christ was the "life of the world." As a result, the Indians of Mexico and Central America use jade extensively in burial masks, beads, pendants, bracelets, etc., as a *symbol* of Quetzalcoatl. (*Christ in America*, p. 119)

Christmas is a holiday set aside to commemorate the birth of Jesus Christ. It is celebrated somewhat differently among Christian nations, but the symbols associated with it are basically the same. First the unborn Christ was turned away from the inn, (Luke 2:7) *as* He would be rejected by His own people later in life. At the time of His birth an angel said to the shepherds "And this shall be a *sign* unto you; Ye shall find the babe wrapped in swaddling clothes lying in a manger." (Luke 2:12) A *sign* meant more than mere directions to find Him; a manger was *symbolically* the lowest place that could be found for his birth. The manger was in *similitude* of the fact that Jesus "descended below all things...that he might be in all and through all things." (D & C 88:6; 122:8) The swaddling clothes in which the baby Jesus was wrapped were strips of cloth used on newborn babies to restrict their movements. Jesus grew out of these material strapings *symbolizing* that he would overcome the material bonds and restrictions placed upon him at mortal birth and that he would ascend above all things. Similarly Christ went down into the waters of baptism and came up out of the water newly born; then at His death He "descended below all things," *symbolized* by the borrowed grave in which he was buried, after which He rose from the grave a resurrected being.

The shepherds to whom the angels appeared at the birth of Christ as they were "keeping watch over their flock by night" (Luke 2:8) *represented* Him as the good and great shepherd who watches over us. (John 10:11; Hebrews 13:20, etc.) The "wise men of the east" (Matthew 2:1-14) must have been on some divine errand of the Eternal Father, for they were guided to the baby Jesus by a star, then "warned by God in a dream that they should return by a different route." The star is a universal *symbol* of the Lord's divine guidance. The gifts they were bearing to Jesus were not ordinary. In their religious use they were to be pure gold, pure frankincense, and pure myrrh, *symbols* of the purity of the Baby to whom the wise men were delivering the gifts. Gold is often used in the scriptures to *symbolize* purity and divinity. Among the places that pure gold was required by the Lord was for the Ark of the Covenant and the mercy seat in the Tabernacle (Exodus 25). The altar vessels, etc. in Solomon's temple were made of, or inlaid with, pure gold. (1 Kings 6:22) Pure frankincense was required, (combined with 3 spices) for the "pure and holy" perfume that was used by the priests to "put of it before the (arc of the) testimony in the Tabernacle of the congregation." Pure myrrh was one of the principle ingredients required for preparing a holy anointing oil. It was used for anointing various things in the Tabernacle, and oil of myrrh was used for "the purifying of the women" for six months of "the days of their purifications" to present themselves to the king. (Exodus 30; Esther 2:12)

The coat of many colors that Jacob made for Joseph had extra *significance* because of the extra love Jacob had for Joseph. (Genesis

37:3) At the time Joseph was sold into Egypt by his brothers, they took the coat their father had made for him and stripped it from Joseph and dipped it into the blood of a kid to make their father believe Joseph had been killed. (Genesis 37:31-33) Afterwards the coat became a *symbol* to the descendants of Joseph, as described by Moroni, commander of the Nephite army: "Let us remember the words of Jacob, before his death, for behold, he saw that a part of the remnant of the coat of Joseph was preserved...And he said—Even as the remnant of the garment of my son hath been preserved, *so shall* a remnant of the seed of my son be preserved by the hand of God." (Alma 46:23-24) Later Ether said that a New Jerusalem should be built upon the remnant of the seed of Joseph, for which there had been a *symbol*. "For as Joseph brought his father out of Egypt...the Lord brought a remnant of the seed of Joseph out of Jerusalem...and they shall build up a holy city unto the Lord, *like unto* the Jerusalem of old." (Ether 13:6-9)

The Lord's Guiding Hand

A *symbol* of the Lord's guiding hand was given to the Children of Israel in the form of a cloud. "And the Lord went before them by day in a pillar of a cloud, to lead them the way; and by night in a pillar of fire, to give them light: to go by day and night." (Exodus 13:21-22; 1 Corinthians 10:2) This cloud was found on other occasions as *representative* of His glory, power and presence. It was with Moses upon the Mount, (Exodus 24:16-17) and covered the tent of the congregation of the Tabernacle, (Exodus 40:34-35) and the Temple. (2 Chronicles 5:13-14; 1 Kings 8:10) The cloud was with Christ, Peter, James, and John at the mount of transfiguration (Matthew 17:5) and was with Christ when He returned to his Father "when a cloud received him out of their sight." (Acts 1:9) The cloud and the glory of the Lord are sometimes used as being synonymous to each other. (1 Kings 8:10-11; 2 Chronicles 5:12-14)

Included in Isaiah's prophecies concerning the latter days is a promise that a cloud will come to the inhabitants of Zion: "And the Lord will create upon every dwelling place of Mount Zion, and upon her assemblies, a cloud and a smoke by day, and the shining of a flaming fire by night." (Isaiah 4:5) At the Kirtland, Ohio temple in the spring of 1836, the glory of the Lord did come to His temple at which time the cloud is not mentioned but the pillar of fire that was prophesied did appear:

> "...when a noise was heard like the sound of a rushing mighty wind, which filled the Temple, and all the congregation simultaneously arose, being moved upon by an invisible power; many began to speak in tongues and prophesy; others saw glorious visions; and I beheld the Temple was filled with angels. The people of the neighborhood came running together (hearing an unusual sound within and seeing a bright light *like* a pillar of fire resting on the Temple)..." (*Temples* 1945, p.23)

The prophecies concerning the second coming of Christ state that He is to come in the clouds of heaven. (Matthew 26:64; Daniel 7:13) In Joseph Smith's translation of Matthew the clouds are represented as one of the *signs* of Jesus Christ. "Then shall appear the *sign* of the Son of Man in heaven, and then shall all the tribes of the earth mourn; and they shall see the Son of Man coming in the clouds of heaven, with power and great glory." (Matthew 24:30) The Lord said that this cloud is going to come to his temple in New Jerusalem, "which cloud shall be even the glory of the Lord, which shall fill the house." (D & C 84:5) From the preceeding scriptures, one can determine that the *symbol* of the cloud often *represents* the Lord and His power when He is not personally on the earth. It is also the *sign* of the Son of Man, one of the symbols by which he will be seen at His coming.

The hand is used as a *symbol* in many early Christian pictures and engravings. The scriptures contain several descriptions of someone sitting or being on the right hand of the Lord or the Father, representing it as a position of prestige or authority. The right hand sometimes *symbolically* represents the priesthood power of the Godhead and the order of authority under which it is administered: "Thy right hand, O Lord, is become glorious in power: thy right hand, O Lord, hath dashed in pieces the enemy." (Exodus 15:6) "Ye shall see the Son of Man sitting on the right of power." (Mark 14:62) "My right hand hath spanned the heavens." (1 Nephi 20:13) According to Elder Joseph Fielding Smith, the right hand was used as a *symbol* of righteousness: (*Answers*, Vol. 1, p. 157) "I am thy God: I will strengthen thee; yea, I will help thee; yea, I will uphold thee with the right hand of my righteousness." (Isaiah 41:10) Jacob crossed his hands in order to give the greater blessing and birthright, through his right hand, to Ephraim instead of Manasseh. (Genesis 48:17-20)

Church members raise the right hand to sustain the general, stake and ward authorities, to sustain members in new church positions, and to approve new members of a ward. Members usually take the sacrament with the right hand, (*Answers,* Vol. 1, p. 154) and usually shake hands with the right hand. The right hand is called the dexter, which is *representative* of something favorable, while the left hand is called the sinister and is *associated* with the unfortunate or perverse. (*Doctrines of Salv.,* Vol. 3, p. 107; *Answers,* Vol. 1, p. 158) Thus the right and left hands are in *similitude* of the basic gospel principle of good in contrast to evil. This principle is supported in Matthew:

> When the Son of Man shall come in his glory...And before him shall be gathered all nations: and he shall separate them one from another as a shepherd divideth his sheep from the goats:
>
> And he shall set the sheep on his right hand, but the goats on the left....
>
> Then shall he say also, unto them on the left hand, depart from me, ye cursed, into everlasting fire, prepared for the devil and his angels. (Matthew 25:31-33, 41; Mosiah 5:12)

The right hand is also used in connection with some ordinances of the gospel, but that does not mean that the left hand is not acceptable where someone is crippled or has lost his right hand. Wherever substitution is necessary, the intent and purpose of the ordinance or covenant should be kept in mind since the principle to be learned is the meaning and purpose of the symbolic representation.

There are several scriptures symbolic of God's power and authority in his relationship between the heavens and the earth wherein the earth is *represented* as His footstool. Sometimes the *symbols* of the right hand and the footstool were combined to *represent* the Lord's power over the earth:

> And he ruleth high in the heavens, for it is his throne, and this earth is his footstool. (1 Nephi 17:39)

Also,

> I have made the earth rich, and behold it is my footstool wherefore again I will stand on it. (D & C 38:17)

And,

> Exalt ye the Lord our God, and worship at his footstool; for
> he is holy. (Psalm 99:5; 132:7)

And also,

> But to which of the angels said He "Sit on my right hand until
> I make thine enemies thy footstool?" (Hebrews 1:13-14)

Numbers Used as Symbols

The number "twelve" plays an important role in the scriptures as
a *symbol* of gospel principles, and there are in the basement of several
of the Latter-day Saint temples a baptismal font resting on twelve
symbolic oxen statues. Many of the emblems comprising the number
twelve point to the Jerusalem which is to be established when the earth
is resurrected. This holy city that John saw in a vision:

> ...had a wall great and high, and had twelve gates, and at the
> gates twelve angels and names written thereon, which are the
> names of the twelve tribes of the children of Israel:...
>
> And the wall of the city had twelve foundations, and in them
> the names of the twelve apostles of the lamb. (Revelation 21:10-14)
>
> And he showed me a pure river of water of life clear as
> crystal...and on either side of the river was there the tree of life
> which bore twelve manner of fruits, and yielded her fruit every
> month; and the leaves of the tree were for the healing of the
> nations. (Revelation 22:1,2)

There are stylized twelve pointed
stars on the outside east and west
doors of the Salt Lake temple and the
early drawings of the Nauvoo temple
shows a different variation. It consists
of a row of designs on the facade
below the roof line with a circle in the
center and twelve scallops around the
outside of each. James Churchward,
a writer about symbols, depicted a
similar symbol but with interlaced

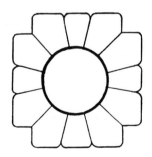

Figure 1

Figure 2

triangles inside the circle. (*Sacred Symbols,* p. 41) He said that there are twelve divisions formed in the spaces between the two interlaced triangles inside the circle. The twelve scallops pictured on the outside of the circle coincide with the divisions. He claimed that the twelve divisions *represent* the gates to heaven and *symbolize* twelve earthly virtues. (Sacred Symbols, p. 140) More appropriately they *symbolize* the twelve gates, foundations, angels, apostles and tribes of the Holy City that St. John described. (Revelation 21:12-14) The design on the Nauvoo temple distinctly separates the scallops with three on each side coinciding with St. John's description of the Holy City as having three gates on each of the east, north, south and west sides.

The Prophet Joseph Smith drew plans in detail for the "City of Zion" that is to be built in Jackson County, Missouri, which is expected to be built at the beginning of the millennium. The plan for the city is designed to contain twelve temples (*Hist. of Church,* Vol. 1, p. 358; *Doctrines of Salv.,* Vol. 3, p. 93) The foundations under the walls of the holy city are to bear the names of the twelve apostles of the Lamb, *representing* the twelve apostles that will sit on twelve thrones and judge the twelve tribes of Israel (Matthew 19:28; D & C 29:12) who hold the keys to open up the authority of God's Kingdom upon the four corners of the earth. (D & C 124:128)

The sacrificial offerings by the children of Israel included several multiples of twelve to *represent* the twelve tribes: There were twelve pillars on the altar, (Exodus 24:4) twelve silver bowls and twelve spoons of gold used at the altars by the princes of Israel, (Numbers 7:84) and the sin offerings included twelve oxen, rams, lambs of the first year, and twelve he-goats, according to the number of the tribes of Israel. (Numbers 7:87; Ezra 6:17)

In the temple of Solomon was built a baptismal font which was called a molten or brazen sea in the Old Testament. It was large in size so that it *represented* the sea in which many are baptized. "And it stood upon twelve oxen, three looking toward the north, three looking toward the west and three looking toward the south and three looking toward the east, and all their hinder parts were inward." (1 Kings, 7:23-25, 44; Jeremiah 52:20) The twelve oxen are *emblematic* of the twelve gates of the holy city and the names of the tribes of Israel written thereon. As each group of three faces one of the cardinal points of the compass, they *represent* each of the three gates of the Holy City in the post-millennial Jerusalem heretofore described.

The All-Seeing Eye

The "All-Seeing Eye" is a common symbol used by many religious and fraternal organizations. It is used by the Masons, Odd Fellows,

Figure 3

Egyptians, Jews, and by the Mormons. It is depicted on the upper part of the east and west windows on the Salt Lake Temple. Originally it had very simple *representations* as suggested by these scriptures: "The eyes of the Lord are in every place beholding the evil and the good." (Proverbs 15:3) "The eyes of the Lord are upon the righteous..." (Psalms 34:15; 1 Peter 3:12) "Yea every knee shall bow, and every tongue confess before him...and shrink beneath the glance of his all-searching eye." (Mosiah 27:31; Psalms 33:18) Brigham Young said the all-searching eye led the Saints from Nauvoo and across the plains to the Great Salt Lake Valley. (*Journal*, Vol. 2, p. 32) To the Babylonians and Assyrians the all seeing eye *symbolized* divine protection; (*Amulets & Talismans*, p. 91) to the Egyptians, it represented God looking down from heaven and the universal vision of the Deity (*Behold The Sign*, p. 43; *Lost Continent* p. 152) It was a common *symbol* of the omniscience of the Father. (*Christian Sym.*, p. 3; *M & Masonry*, p. 62) "Behold the eye of the Lord is on them that fear him..." (Psalm 33:18) In early Christian chapels a picture of the eye was sometimes inscribed inside an equilateral triangle or circle set in such a position that it might look down on the congregation with stern disapproval. The triangle *represented* the trinity with the eye looking out from heaven. This symbol was popular in the days of the three-decker pulpits and three-hour sermons. (*Church Sym.*, p. 50)

The eye as a symbol was discovered to be of significant use hundreds of years before Christ, as attested by the enormous numbers of Udgat amulets found in the tombs of Egypt. Mr. Wallis Budge believes the Egyptians, like the Chinese, were terrified by some "Evil Eye and that the Udgat amulet was worn as a protection against it." (*Amulets,* p. 142) The early Jews used what they called the "much suffering eye" or "sound eye." It is pictured on the back of a "Seal of Solomon" and other amulets worn by very early Jewish tribe members. This "much-suffering" eye is pictured with the eye being torn or with a tear on the side of it. Mr. Goodenough says it was supposedly used as a protection against the evil eye and also on buildings to *remind* the Jews of the eye of the Lord being upon them. The regular eye symbol was supposed to *represent* the "sound eye," then as it was shown torn it was a *symbol* of the Lord being torn by the forces of evil and His suffering and then being restored. (*Jewish Symbols*, Vol.2, pp. 238-239)

Figure 4

Chapter Three

MISCELLANEOUS GEOMETRIC SYMBOLS

The LDS Church's Claim on Symbols

Many historians think that the lines, curves and angles that are used to form squares, circles, triangles, stars, and other geometric forms were the earliest forms of symbolic messages, some of them extending beyond Egyptian history. Notwithstanding their absence from Bible scripture they form the basis for extensive projections of gospel principle to the human mind. Some of the geometric symbols were given in an address by the late Herman R. Bangerter and were published in *Temples of The Most High* (1940's editions). Mr. Bangerter was a member of the Rosicrucian Order, a brotherhood claiming to have existed for 3,500 years. He told me that the material in the article was compiled from the Rosicrucian library.

Geometrical Symbols

Sometimes tourists wonder why the six-pointed Star of David is on the Latter-day Saint Church Assembly Hall in Salt Lake City, and why the five-pointed star, the clasped hands, and the all-seeing eye are on the Salt Lake Temple. They ask why these have been used by the Mormons as symbols, when they thought these symbols belonged to the Jews, the Masons, or to some other religion or fraternity. The Church of Jesus Christ of Latter-day Saints teaches the same gospel as was established by the Lord during his ministry on earth. It is the same gospel as was revealed to Adam and all the Old Testament Prophets. Therefore, the Church has a very direct claim to any of the gospel symbols that were revealed to the early prophets.

The Cross, Circle and Square

The cross is probably the most common of the geometric and design symbols and one of the oldest. It is found on ancient amulets and talismans and in old Egyptian and

Babylonian records. One historian thought that it might have been used as a *sign* to the Egyptians of an *allusion* to the future coming of Christ, but others have refuted this idea as the evidence shows it to have other meanings. Before Christ, the T-type cross was a *symbol* of a hammer or borer depicting the idea of a grinder or an avenger. (*Migration of Sym.*, p. 15) Many protestant churches

Figure 5

use a cross to *symbolize* the crucifixion of Jesus Christ, but the cross was not used as a crucifix until after the fourth century A.D. when Constantine had it placed on the shields of his soldiers. The form of the cross was changed about that time to resemble the T cross, but with the cross bar placed below the top to *represent* the crucifixion of Christ. However it did not appear in or on churches until the seventh or eighth century. (*Amulets*, p. 350)

Figure 6

Drawings and paintings of Christ on the cross began about the fifth century after Christ, but the figures were fully clothed until after the eleventh century, after which His clothing was gradually *represented* by a loin cloth. In the same way, up until the fourteenth century the baby Jesus was always *depicted* clothed. But after this period, as a result of the decadence of Christian art, He is *represented* naked, or nearly so. (*Amulets*, p. 350) The artists did not, nor do they now, show the swaddling clothes that Jesus was wrapped in as a newborn baby, although they have deep symbolic significance.

The General Authorities of The Church of Jesus Christ of Latter-day Saints have resisted the use of the crucifixion cross as a symbol on their churches or as a clothing accessory because it has become commercialized, and many individuals and various Christian churches have come to idolize it. Many people wear the cross on pendants around their neck or on their wrists as charms that are supposed to have mystical and religious powers. Some kiss them in adoration while others include them in their adoration and prayers, thus making the cross a form of idol worship.

The most common cross before Christ had equal arms and several *meanings*. It was *symbolic* of heaven or of the four corners of heaven and a *sign* of divine protection, riches, prosperity and life. (*Amulets,* pp. 96, 338-339) Church-ward said the cross represents what he calls the Sacred Four powers or forces that executed the commands of the creator during the creation of the earth. (*Lost Continent*, pp. 33, 162; *Sacred Sym.,* p. 71) However to me the four great powers or pillars of the universe are the creation, fall, atonement and resurrection. According to modern day revelation there "are four angels sent forth from God to whom is given power over the four parts of the earth, to save life and to destroy;..." (D & C 77:8; Revelation 7:1) Also the cross could *represent* the four beasts spoken of by John in the book of Revelation: "Heaven, the paradise of God, the happiness of man, and of beasts...to *represent* the glory of the classes of beings in their destined order or sphere of creation;..." (D & C 77:2-3; Revelation 4:6) In China the earth is *represented* to have been made in the form of a cross. (*Migration of Sym.,* p. 14)

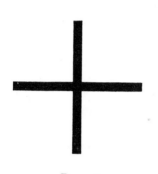

Figure 7

The circle, which is endless, is a *symbol* of perfection. (*Temples* p. 240) Without beginning nor end, the circle teaches the cultured mind the meaning of infinity, (*Lost Continent,* p. 138)

Figure 8

and of never-ending existence. (*Signs and Symbols,* p. 275) An old Egyptian Papyrus states "If we live on we must continue forever, and if we continue forever, like the circle and eternity man had no beginning." (*Sacred Sym.,* p. 156) M.A. Pottenger lists the circle as a *"symbol* of Divinity—the infinite, perfect mind, which is limitless, boundless and which includes within itself all real things." (*M and Masonry,* p. 61) Since all of the Father's dominion is eternal and endless, the circle is a symbol of the universe without beginning or end, and of eternal life within the universe. (Ralph M. Lewis, *Behold the Sign,* p. 43) A picture of the sun is sometimes used to represent the circle

Figure 9

as a symbol and as such is depicted on the stones of Polynesian ruins and on the walls of buildings in many ancient lands. (*Lost Continent,* p. 138) Originally the sun was to be regarded as a symbol and not to be worshipped although it represented Deity. In Edwin R. Goodenough's volumes of Jewish Symbols are several designs of endless interwoven spirals without an explanation of their significance. (*Jewish Symbols,* Vol.3, Fig. 640) Churchward says that since there is no starting or ending points in such spirals, they are equivalent of a circle and are an ancient reference to man's soul having no beginning nor end and that these symbols were generally found associated with the passing of the soul in burial chambers. (*Sacred Symbols,* pp. 156-157)

The square was considered inferior to the circle and as such was used to *symbolize* the earth and earth's existence. (*Signs & Symbols,* pp. 269, 276; *Sacred Sym.,* p. 157) The four corners *represented* the four cardinal points—north, south, east and west.

Figure 10

(*Lost Continent,* p. 143) The scriptures refer to the earth as having four quarters or corners. (Ether 13:11; Revelation 7:1) On the four corners or walls of a square building the exact measurements *symbolize* the divine order (*Funk & Wagnalls Company,* p. 1096) building uprightly on a strong secure foundation. (*Temples,* p. 240) The perfect square, as with the perfect circle, comprises 360 degrees, symbolically perfection. Because the circle *represents* eternity and the divine perfection of the Father and Son, and the square *represents* the earth and earth life, both of them combined would be a *symbol* of mankind striving to be perfect even as his Father in heaven is perfect as commanded by the Lord. (Matthew 5:48; 3 Nephi 12:48) The combined circle and square are often depicted in ancient drawings and carvings.

The Stars as Symbols

A common symbol found among ancient records, synagogues, etc., is the eight pointed star made by interlacing two squares. (*Jewish Symbols,* Vol. 7, p. 198; Vol. 1, p. 212, Figure 547) According to Webber and Goldsmith, the eight-pointed star *signifies* man's regeneration. (*Church Sym.,* p. 26; *Life Symbols,* p. 418) Churchward claims that to the

Figure 11

Egyptians it *represented* the eight roads to heaven to "show man how he must live on this earth to be prepared to pass into the world beyond."

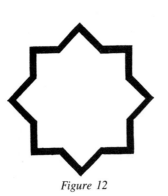

Figure 12

(*Sacred Sym.,* p. 154) He named the roads as right belief, speech, meditations, etc., but these are too general and there are many abstract terms that are more or less equally important. A more logical symbol would have been that one square *represented* faith, repentance, baptism, and the gift of the Holy Ghost, while the other *represented* the Lord's four basic principles of the gospel: study, prayer, service and free agency. Upon these eight basic principles are the roads to heaven by which man is regenerated.

Many of the keystones of the windows and doors in the Salt Lake City LDS Temple are engraved with five-pointed stars. There were some on the LDS Temple at Nauvoo, as well as many buildings of other religions. Most writers attribute the five-pointed star as a *symbol* pointing to the coming of the Savior, based on the prophecy "There shall come a star out of Jacob;..." (Numbers 24:17) and on the Lord's words "I am the root of the offspring of David and the bright and morning star." (Revelation 22:16) The prophecy was fulfilled when the star appeared in Bethlehem

Figure 13

on the night of the birth of Jesus. It is called the Star of the East and the Star of Bethlehem and is a *symbol* of divine guidance. (*Our Christian Sym.*, p. 59; *Signs & Symbols,* p. 59) Funk and Wagnalls Company lists the star as the dawn of hope and the five-pointed star of perfection. (*Funk & Wagnalls Company*, pp. 1095-1096)

According to an article by Herman R. Bangerter:

> The five-pointed star as the lesser seal of Solomon initiates the individual into the mysteries of Godliness....After meditation and instruction they become adept and then as they master the gospel they become priests and priestesses after the order of Melchizedek and as they master the spiritual laws they advance to the six-pointed star, or the great seal of Solomon, where the physical and spiritual become inseparably connected, in the Celestial Kingdom of eternal life. (*Temples*, p. 242)

Triangles and Their Variations

The equilateral triangle is a symbol that has acquired many meanings. Foremost of these is a *representation* of the Father, Son and Holy Ghost as the Godhead or Trinity, *signifying* that they are unified as one in purpose. (*Signs and Symbols,* p. 276; *Church Sym.*, p. 40) Some writers attribute the three equal sides united in one figure as *representing* the false pagan and Christian dogma that the Godhead only consists of one divine essence. There are three separate sides to the triangle *symbolizing* three separate and distinct heavenly beings, who are equal only to the extent that they are all three necessary to one single purpose. (John 17:11; Romans 12:5) The equilateral triangle has many oher symbolic meanings attributed to it. It also *symbolizes* light, life, and love as attributes of the Godhead. (*Life Symbols*, p. 331) It is also regarded by some as a *symbol* of the birth, life and death of mortal man. (*Amulets,* p. 429) Others regard it as a *symbol* of man's rebirth by water, spirit and blood; and also of the body, mind, and spirit. (*Funk & Wagnalls Company,* p. 1096) In

representing the family, the triangle is considered a *symbol* of the father, mother and child: "the first the male principle, the second the female and the third the offspring of the other two, but the three blended into one." (*Life Symbols*, pp. 323-324) With this union in mind "Plato used the triangle as a *symbol* of marriage." (*Life Symbols*, pp. 331-333) Goldsmith *symbolized* the equilateral triangle as

Figure 14

the "Law of Life" and "the completed whole of life," (*Life Symbols*, pp. 323, 336) and Aristotle the "triad as the number of the complete whole." (*Life Symbols,* p. 330) According to the Lord, the family unit cannot enjoy a completed, whole life without being united through celestial marriage and inheriting eternal life. (D & C 131:1-4)

The position in which triangles are placed displays additional representations. With the apex pointing down it was an *emblem* of life flowing from the Creator, (*Pagan,* p. 117) and a divine plane that "*symbolizes* God's consciousness is focalized on mankind." (*Temples,* p. 240) With the apex pointing up, it was an *emblem* of the passive principles received from the Creator, and of a material plane with mankind focusing his thoughts on God. (*Pagan and Christian,* pp. 117-118)

Figure 15

Inman Goldsmith and other non-LDS authors on symbolism wrote some definitions that are interesting to members of The Church of Jesus Christ of Latter-day Saints. They stated that the triangle with its apex pointed upward *signified* the male creator, and with the apex downward, the female, and when the triangles are superimposed to form the six point star, "the idea embodied being the androgyne nature of the Deity" or "the union of the male and female creators." (*Pagan and Christian,* pp. 32, 89; *Life Symbols,* p. 437; *Behold the Sign,* p. 70) "An Androgyne nature occurs when there are both staminate (male) and pistillate (female) flowers in the same cluster with the male being uppermost." (*Webster's Dictionary*) Among the Hindus and Greeks it *signifies* the union of the male and female creators. (*Pagan and Christian,* p. 89)

These definitions are interesting because the world's Christian religions universally do not accept God the Father as having a female partner. The Lord, through The Church of Jesus Christ, has revealed that the Father does have a wife, and because of the priesthood the Father holds, He is uppermost. With the male and female symbols in mind, as the triangles are brought together to form the interlaced triangles, they can *symbolize* the Father and Mother in heaven as being one in unity of purpose and equal partners as Eternal Parents. The term "uppermost" is

Figure 16

used here in a similar sense as Webster uses it in his definition of the "androgyne nature." The fact that the male element is uppermost in the flower does not make the female element less important than the male, for there would be no flowers without both. The fact that the Eternal Father is head of the family in the Celestial Kingdom does not make the Eternal Mother less important than Him.

Neither the husband nor the wife can be exalted in the celestial kingdom without the other, nor can the Eternal Father have spiritual offspring without His eternal companion. Parley P. Pratt said that he learned from the Prophet Joseph Smith "that the highest dignity of womanhood was to stand as a queen and priestess to her husband, and to reign forever and ever as the queen mother of her numerous and still increasing offspring." (*Autobiography of Parley P. Pratt*, Deseret Book Co., 1963, p. 298) A queen and priestess in mortality only partially *symbolizes* the highest position of womanhood since a king can rule without a queen in an earthly kingdom and she is not an equal partner, as will be the queens of the celestial glory.

The Interlaced Triangle or Star of David

The two triangles forming the interlaced triangle or six-pointed star is usually called the Star of David, the Shield of Solomon, Solomon's Seal, or the Creator's Star. (*M & Masonry*, p. 70; *Church Sym.*, p. 43; *Amulets*, p. 223; *Life Symbols*, p. 437; *Christian Sym.*, p. 3) Although it is generally considered a Jewish Symbol (*Jewish Symbols*, Vol. 7, pp. 198-199), it is found among many other religious and secular groups in countries throughout the world.

To some, the six points on the star *represent* the six days of the week (*M & Masonry*, p. 69), while the Adamites claim the points *represent* the creation in six days, (*Amulets*, p. 432) which reinforces the claim that it is the Creator's Star. Although it is doubtful that they were created

Figure 17

as symbols, it is interesting to note that all common snowflake crystals have six points, and are each shaped like a six-pointed star, though each has a different design. There are several star-shaped crystals in each snowflake.

When the two triangles of the six-pointed star are interlaced into one unit, they combine the symbolic ideas they individually represent. The union of the two *symbolizes* the spiritual plane or life of the heavens becoming united with the material plane or life of mankind. (*Life Symbols*, p.334) One triangle is a *symbol* of perfection in the spiritual world and universe; the other of perfection in the physical aspects, and combined they become the six-pointed star, "a *symbol* of the unity of both phases of existence of which man is aware." (Ralph M. Lewis, *Behold the Sign*, p. 46) Herman R. Bangerter adds:

"The square and the interlaced triangles are the only two equiangular and equilateral figures the sum of whose exterior angles equals 360 degrees, or perfection, as *symbolized* by the circle. From these *symbols*, we learn that by building uprightly on a strong secure foundation, we unite the physical and the spiritual, and with them inseparably connected, as *symbolized* by the interlaced triangles, we have eternal life." (*Temples*, 1945, pp. 240-241)

Some Jewish historians have suggested that the Urim and Thummim consisted of two crystals each in the form of a triangle, (*M & Masonry*, p. 69) but a painting commissioned by Brigham Young in 1862 that was on the east wall of the chapel in the Bountiful First Ward illustrated an ordinary pair of spectacles. The painting has been moved to the Church Museum at 46 South West Temple in Salt Lake City, Utah. The Prophet Joseph Smith's mother said that the Urim and Thummin "consisted of two smooth three-cornered diamonds set in glass, and the glasses were set in silver bows which were connected the same way as old-fashioned spectacles." (*The Urim and Thummim*, by Arch S. Reynolds, Springville, Utah, 1950, p. 10) Joseph Smith described them as "two stones in silver bows—and these stones fastened to a breastplate." (Joseph Smith—History 1:35) What the Urim and Thummim consisted of, or in what particular shape they were formed, is not as important as the fact that they were *symbols* of the actual means and power by which they functioned.

Abbreviation and Combination of Symbols

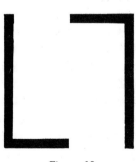

Figure 18

Symbols are an abbreviated form of the idea that they represent and they themselves are often abbreviated. "For in ancient symbols a part of a *symbol* stands for the whole." (*Pagan and Christian*, p. 123) Some of these are: If an angle is taken from one corner of the square, it becomes an "L" or the *sign* of the square; while an angle taken from one of the points of the interlaced triangle becomes a

"V", or the *sign* of the compass.
(Bangerter, *Temples*, 1945, p. 241; See
pictures: *Jewish Symbols*, Vol. 8, Fig.
168) The two-sided square "L" is a
sign of a builder. (*Lost Continent,* p.
149) As an abbreviated square it is a
symbol of justice and uprightness, to
act uprightly, justly and truthful;
(*Sacred Symbols*, p. 136) and an
emblem of morality, which taught the
initiated to square their lives and
actions according to the laws of God.

Figure 19

(*M & Masonry,* p. 60) According to one writer, the square and compass
combined is to teach the people to square their actions and keep them
within due bounds, and another says the compass is the boundary of
passion. (*M and Masonry*, p. 60)

The union of the two equilateral triangles is sometimes illustrated
by inverting one and placing it above the other with the apexes touching
in the center, (See Figure 15) thus forming a double pyramid instead
of interlacing the triangles. According to the Egyptians, this form was
called a double pyramid and *signified* the union of fire and water. (*Life
Symbols,* p. 324; *Pagan and Christian*, pp. 38-39) Since fire is a *symbol*

Figure 20

of the Holy Ghost, the double
pyramid would *represent* the
ordinance when a person is baptized
with fire and the Holy Ghost as is
performed in The Church of Jesus
Christ of Latter-day Saints. If the top
and bottom horizontal bars are
removed, it forms an abbreviated "X"
as is found on the margins of the
Isaiah portion of the Dead Sea Scrolls
(Solomon Zeitlin, *Dead Sea Scrolls
and Modern Scholarship*, p. 54), and
among many ancient American glyphs. Goodenough's books on *Jewish
Symbols* have illustrations of them on seals dated as early as 3,000 B.C.
This symbol refers to the active and passive elements in nature (*Lost
Continent,* pp. 204-205) and the merging of the physical and the spiritual

preparatory to forming the interlaced triangles. (*Temples,* p. 241) Thus, according to the similarities of its *representations* of the interlaced triangles, it is an abbreviation of the six-pointed star. The "X" is often abbreviated with a straight line. A straight line is without blemish, therefore, an *emblem* of the absolute truth, and is often used as a ceremonial bar among symbols of the ancestors of the American Indians. (*Tree of Life Symbols,* p. 122; *M. & Masonry,* p. 62; *Lost Continent* p. 124)

Figure 21

Not only is the Tree of Life an important concept in the scriptures, it is found in almost every location and religion where symbols were used. It was placed in the Garden of Eden as being beyond mankind while in mortality. (Genesis 3:22; Moses 4:28; Alma 42:5) Not only does the Bible mention fruit on the tree, but the Jews, Chaldeans and others depicted fruit on their drawings. The designs are many and vary, from very crude sketches to the Jewish Menorah; some of them are simple; others are combined with triangles and other geometric drawings. A stela found in Mexico had the tree of life carved on it in such a way as to illustrate Lehi's dream as recorded in the Book of Mormon. (*Archaeology,* p. 103) An angel described the tree of life in Lehi's dream as *symbolizing* the love of God. (1 Nephi 8:21-22)

The number seven is prominently used in the scriptures. By combining the four sides of the square with the three sides of a triangle, the number seven combines the symbolic representations of the square and the triangle. There are seven days of the week in *remembrance* of the seven days of the earth's creation. Clean beasts entered the Ark "by sevens." (Genesis 7:2) As a *sign* of perfect submission as the Savior did to His Father, Jacob "bowed himself to the ground seven times" before Esau when the two met for a reconciliation. (Genesis 33:3) He served Laban seven years twice in order for Leah and Rachel to be his wives. (Genesis 29:16-30) In the dream of Pharaoh which Joseph interpreted, the seven full ears *represented* seven years of plenty. The seven thin ears *represented* seven years of famine. (Genesis 41:22-30) According to the Lord's command, Joshua and his army marched around the city of Jericho for seven days led by seven priests blowing seven trumpets, and they compassed the city seven times on the seventh day, at which time the walls fell. (Joshua 6:2-20) John saw a book which was sealed with seven seals, containing "the revealed will, mysteries, and the works of God...concerning the earth during the seven thousand years of its existence." (D & C 77:6; Revelation 5:1) When the seventh seal was opened preceding the second coming of Christ, John saw "...the seven angels which stood before God; and to them were given seven trumpets." (Revelation 8:1-2) "And the sounding of the trumpets of the seven angels are the preparing and finishing of his work, in the beginning of the seventh thousand years." (D & C 77:12)

The Lord commanded Moses to make a candlestick with three branches on each side and one on top, totaling seven. (Exodus 25:31-32) The Menorah, used in Jewish temples and found on many Jewish Artifacts, had seven uniform branches, three on each side and one on top, and was in the form of both a candlestick and a tree. Instead of holding candles, the menorah had cups on the ends of the seven branches that contained pure olive oil in which a wick was inserted. The menorah originally *symbolized* a tree, and the buds sometimes illustrated on it were to *represent* the leaves or fruit on a tree. Later, the buds consisted

Figure 22

of cups to hold olive oil and a wick. To some the menorah was a *symbol* of life or the tree of life, while to others it simply indicated "the Law by which a Jew hoped to be saved." (*Jewish Symbols*, Vol. 4, pp. 72-78) The burning of the olive oil in the menorah would *symbolize* the light and guidance from the Holy Spirit, much the same as when the ten wise virgins lit their lamps. (D & C 45:57) According to Ernst Lehner, it was a *symbol* of perfection which is necessary for a person to attain if he is to fully partake of the fruit of the tree of life. (*Picture Book,* pp. 36-37; *New Bible Dictionary,* p. 898)

Several ancient rough drawings indicate that the artists were attempting to combine the symbolic meaning of the seven-branch tree or menorah with those of geometric symbols. One shows the tree with a square at its base and with an X inside the square forming up-and-

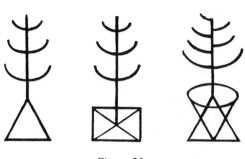

Figure 23

down pointing triangles with the apexes touching. (*Jewish Symbols*, Vol. 3, Fig. 719) Another drawing illustrates a less formal tree setting in a cone with the up-and-down parts of the X supporting a circle. (*Jewish Symbols*, Vol. 5, Fig. 32) Another shows a triangle as the base of a tree. Yet another pictured a circle which *represents* the all-seeing eye, having as its base up and down pointing triangles. (*The Lost Language*, Vol. 2, p. 169) A tree form published by Harold Baley in 1912 shows double "V's." He said that among the Greeks and in India they *symbolized* twins who were celestial children of the creator and were regarded as lords of light and conquerors of darkness. (*The Lost Language*, Vol. 1, pp. 14-15) The double V is at the center of the stem of the diagram. A square forms the base with a cross inside and an X is at the top of the stem.

Figure 24

The square base is set with a corner on the bottom end so the angles would form up and down pointing triangles. Between the double V and square there is a straight line. Much meaning could be read into this single *symbol*.

The Star of David that is on the assembly hall at Temple Square in Salt Lake City has a lot more symbolism than is generally supposed. The interlaced triangles are quite obvious but in the center is a circle with its symbolism. Inside the circle is a square superimposed with a four-petal rosette which was commonly used as a square, thus forming interlaced squares. Similar designs were used in the Graco-Roman period. (*Jewish Sym.*, Vol. 2, p. 14) Inside each of the triangles points of the Star of David is a three-pointed rosette which is a styliz-

Figure 25: Star of David (interlaced triangles) on Assembly Hall, square with overlaid rosette, square inside eternity circle, rosette triangle inside triangle of 6-points of star.

ed triangle. Outside the star are life-giving vines which are explained in the final chapter.

The symbols illustrated and explained up to this point have been selected from many others available because they more fully reflect the principles of God's plan of salvation. The ideas behind them will enhance the following discussions concerning man's place in the universe.

Chapter Four

THE ETERNAL NATURE
OF THE UNIVERSE

The Importance of Knowledge Concerning the Universe

The universe consists of God's creations with His power and jurisdiction over them. It includes numerous worlds prepared for His spirit children who enter the earth's sphere as mortal beings.

A knowledge of the nature and scope of the universe is important in order to understand the manner of and purpose for which God uses *symbols* to prepare mankind to return to His realm. The reader should keep in mind a basic principle of symbolism that the Lord has revealed, which is "that all things may have their *likeness*, and that they may accord one with the other,...that which is earthly conforming to that which is heavenly." (D&C 128:13) In other words, the major part of gospel symbolism will show a relationship between the two realms— the earthly things will point toward the heavenly.

An Infinite Universe

According to the doctrine of The Church of Jesus Christ of Latter-day Saints, the expanding universe had no beginning, nor will it have an end. However, insofar as the scriptures and this book is concerned, they are speaking of and dealing with matter pertaining to this earth upon which mankind dwells. (Moses 1:40) The concept of a perpetual universe is supported by many scientists including Raymond A. Lyttleton:

Only the elements that go to make up the universe have finite ages, that is the galaxies themselves. The universe itself had no beginning and no end. It would not matter where in the universe the observer happened to be; he would be able to regard himself as the center of it, and find all other galaxies streaming away from him. Although change is going on everywhere, the general overall situation always remains very much the same. As it was in the beginning, is now and ever shall be: the world without end. (*Modern Universe*, pp. 203-204; see also *Nature of Universe*, pp. 111-112)

From the statement in the Bible that the earth before its creation was without form and void, many theologians argue that God created the earth out of nothing, but such is not true. He formed this earth out of material floating in space: the gas, dust, hydrogen, and other large and small materials. How long had this material been in existence? Joseph Smith said: "The pure principles of element are principles that can never be destroyed; they may be organized and reorganized, but never destroyed. They had no beginning and can have no end." (*Teachings*, p. 351)

People look at the sky and see the "Milky Way," which is the core of a giant system of millions of stars called a galaxy, in which our sun is on the outer edge. Some of the bright dots one sees are not stars, but are other galaxies which are part of systems of galaxies, and these systems are part of still larger systems. These galaxies and systems are receding from each other at tremendous speeds and new stars and systems are forming in the space left between them from the material throughout space. (*Realm of Nebulae*, p. 82; *Modern Universe*, pp. 28, 181, 203; *Nature of Universe*, p.69)

Many years before astronomers were proposing an expanding universe as they now visualize it, Latter-day Saint Church leaders were describing it. Parley P. Pratt (martyred in 1867) prophesied that in future years "The heavens will multiply and new worlds and more people will be added to the kingdoms of the Fathers, thus, in the progress of events unnumbered millions of worlds and systems of worlds will necessarily be called into requisition." (*Key to Theology*, pp. 53-54) Of these systems the Lord told Abraham that there are many stars in the heavens some of which are governing ones, that the greatest of all is called Kolob which governs those of a lower order, and "that Kolob is *after the manner* of the Lord." (Abraham 3:2-16) The *Doctrine and Covenants* referred to these systems as kingdoms: "And there are many kingdoms; and there is no kingdom in which there is no space, either a greater or lesser kingdom. And unto every kingdom is given a law and unto every law there are certain bounds, also, and conditions." (D & C 88:37-38, recorded in 1833)

Priesthood the Governing Power

Most people believe that there is some kind of supreme power that governs the universe and the kingdoms within it. Brigham Young said:

> There is a Power that has organized all things from the crude matter that floats in the immensity of space. He has given form, motion, and life to this material world; has made the great and small lights that bespangle the firmament above....He has caused the air and water to team with life, and covered the hills and plains with creeping things.
>
> All these wonders are the work of the Almighty Ruler of the universe, in whom we believe and whom we worship....God is the source, the fountain of all intelligence, no matter who possesses it. (*Discourses of Young*, p. 18)

The Lord says: "For behold, there are many worlds that have passed away by the word of my power. And there are many that now stand, and innumerable are they unto man." (Moses 1:35) What is the "word of his power" with which He created the earth and His many creations? How can He be above all things, and in all things, and through all things, and round about all things (D & C 88:41), inasmuch as He is not everywhere at the same time? The answer is in the power by which God governs and operates, which power He calls priesthood. President John Taylor wrote of the priesthood:

> It is the government of God, whether on the earth or in the heavens; for it is by that power, agency or principle that all things are governed on earth and in the heavens, and by that power all things are upheld and sustained. It governs all things—it directs all things—it sustains all things—and has to do with all things that God and truth are associated with.

God has organized a priesthood, and that priesthood bears rule in all things pertaining to the earth and the heavens; one part of it exists in the heavens, another part on earth; they both cooperate together for...the redemption of the dead and the living. (*Millennial Star*, Vol. 9, Nov. 1, 1847, pp. 321, 323)

Brigham Young said, concerning the priesthood: "It is the law by which the worlds are, were, and will continue forever and ever. It is that system which brings the worlds into existence and peoples them...." (*Discourses of Young*, p. 130)

Priesthood is the power or substance which gives life to all things. Without it man would have no power to cause airplanes to fly, electricity to supply homes or industry, or machines to move mountains, or autos to run. In short, it enables all powers of a lesser or earthly nature to operate.

The Nature of the Godhead and Mankind

The ruling body of the universe, insofar as this earth is concerned, consists of a Godhead—the Eternal Father, His Son, and the Holy Ghost. They are three separate and distinct beings. Christ states, "I and my Father are one," but He also asks of the Father that the twelve apostles "may be one as we are." They are one "in purpose," in that they created, control and direct the earth and all that dwell thereon. As an illustration, a few years ago two reporters visited Mustang, a small kingdom with ancient customs dating back to Biblical times, in order to write a story of their history and customs. The king said to those he assigned to accompany them through the kingdom: "I request that these two foreigners, *who are one person*, should be allowed assistance in my realm." (*National Geographic*, Oct. 1965, p. 592) The custom of calling two or more individuals "one" had been carried down from the time that the Godhead were called "one" as recorded in the New Testament.

The Doctrine & Covenants says of the Godhead that "The Father has a body of flesh and bones as tangible as man's; the Son also; but the Holy Ghost has not a body of flesh and bones, but is a personage of spirit." (D & C 130:22)

In Christ's antemortal existence He was literally the spirit child of the Eternal Father, Elohim. All of mankind were spirit children of our

Heavenly Father and Mother. Describing the origin of man, Joseph Fielding Smith declared that Jesus

> ...is the Firstborn of all the sons of God—the First begotten in the spirit and the Only Begotten in the flesh. He is our elder brother, and we, like Him, are in the image of God. All men and women are in the *similitude* of the universal Father and Mother, and we are literally sons and daughters of Deity.
>
> God created man in His own image! This is just as true of the spirit as it is of the body, which is only the clothing of the spirit; the two together constituting the soul. The spirit of man is in the form of man and the spirits of all creatures are in the *likeness* of their bodies. (*Origin and Destiny*, pp. 351-352; see also D&C 77:2)

Although the spirit body is in the same form or shape as the physical body, it is composed of a different material. The Prophet Joseph said: "There is no such thing as immaterial matter. All spirit is matter, but it is more refined and pure and can only be seen by purer eyes. We cannot see it; but when our bodies are purified we shall see that it is all matter." (D & C 131:7-8)

In summary, the universe has neither a beginning nor end. It is composed of systems of planets, stars and suns within millions of galaxies and systems of galaxies that are receding from each other at tremendous speeds. Within the space between them are created new worlds, suns and galaxies, all of which are created and controlled by the power of the priesthood, under the power and authority of God or Gods. To Eternal parents are born countless spirit children to inhabit these new systems.

The Purpose of God's Creations

With recent scientific discoveries, men and women have traveled to the moon and have built satellites upon which they circle the earth. Scientists are now projecting huge satellites upon which hundreds of people will be born, live and die while orbiting other planets at great distances from here. This chapter describes even greater possibilities of achievement for those who attain the celestial kingdom after resurrection.

As recorded in the *Pearl of Great Price*, the Father revealed the purpose for which he created the universe and raised millions of spirit children: "And worlds without number have I created; and I also created them for mine own purpose; and by the Son I created them, which is mine only Begotten....For behold, this is my work and my glory— to bring to pass the immortality and eternal life of man." (Moses 1:33, 39)

In the pre-mortal life the Father's spirit children were taught and given experiences in a variety of ways to develop their knowledge and capabilities in preparation for their mortal existence; this mortal privilege is based upon their obedience to the Eternal Father in the pre-mortal estate. They were "born of heavenly parents and reared to maturity, in the eternal mansions of the Father, prior to coming upon the earth in a temporal body to undergo an experience in mortality." (*Origin and Destiny*, p. 354)

Degrees in God's Realm

Likewise mankind on earth is instructed in the laws and principles of God and the universe, and he experiences those things that can enable him to develop the capabilities which may prepare him to return to the Father's Kingdom. Depending on his worthiness and capabilities, he will inherit a place in one of the many mansions of the Eternal Father. (Ether 12:32) The Lord said, "In my Father's house are many mansions...I go to prepare a place for you...that where I am, there ye may be also." (John 14:2) Earthly homes range from small huts to elaborate estates; *likewise*, there will be a great differences between the abodes of resurrected beings and between the types of immortal life they will merit. In the Father's Kingdom there are three heavens or glories: (2 Corinthians 12:2)

> There are celestial bodies, and bodies terrestrial; but the glory of the celestial is one, and the glory of the terrestrial is another. There is one glory of the sun, and another glory of the moon, and another glory of the stars: for one star differeth from another star in glory. *So also* is the resurrection of the dead. (1 Corinthians 15:40-42)

The sun, moon and stars are *symbolic* of the degrees of glory and variety of rewards or places of abode or inheritance destined for mankind. Following are a few excerpts from a vision received by the prophet Joseph Smith about the three degrees of heavenly glory. Describing those who will enter the celestial kingdom the Lord revealed:

> They are they unto whose hands the Father has given all things—
> They are they who are priests and kings; who have received of his fullness, and of his Glory....
> These shall dwell in the presence of God and Christ forever and ever....
> These are they whose bodies are celestial, whose glory the sun of the firmament is written of as being *typical*. (D & C 76:55, 62, 70)
> And again, we saw the terrestrial world, and behold and lo, these are they who are of the terrestrial, whose glory differs from that of the church of the Firstborn who have received the fullness of the Father *even as* that of the moon differs from the sun in the firmament....
> These are they who receive of his glory, but not of his fullness....
> These are they who receive of the presence of the Son, but not of the fullness of the Father.
> Wherefore, they are bodies terrestrial, and not bodies celestial and differ in glory *as the* moon differs from the sun. (D & C 76:71, 76, 77, 78)
> And again we saw the glory of the telestial, which glory is that of the lesser, *even as* the glory of the stars differ from that of the glory of the moon in the firmament....
> These are they who receive not of his fullness in the eternal world, but of the Holy Spirit through the ministration of the terrestrial.
> And also the telestial receive it of the administering of angels who are appointed to minister for them, or who are appointed to be ministering spirits for them; for they shall be heirs of salvation....(D & C 76:81, 85-88, 109, 112)

The three degrees of kingdoms of glory are all part of the Father's realm and *typify* the difference in degree of attainment and enjoyment to be received by mankind in postmortal life. Very little is revealed as to where the terrestrial and telestial kingdoms are located or what level of life those who enter them will enjoy, except that those who inherit only a lesser kingdom will be deprived of many of the privileges of the celestial glory. There will be great disappointment and remorse for the loss of opportunities that might have been theirs had they inherited celestial glory. (Alma 40:26; 41:4; D & C 19:6) Of such a loss Elder Ballard said: "If I should be so unfortunate as to lose my chance of obtaining an inheritance in that place,...I surely will feel the full force of the poet's statement, 'Of all sad words of tongue and pen, the saddest are these, it might have been.'" (*Sermons* p. 259)

Who and What is God

The Celestial Kingdom is the abode of God and Christ and all those who inherit a place in His kingdom. They "shall inherit thrones, kingdoms, principalities, and powers, dominions, all heights and depths." (D & C 132:19) Paul declared "that we are the children of God: and if children then heirs; heirs of God and joint heirs with Christ; if so be that we suffer with him, that we may also be glorified together." (Romans 8:16, 17) The *Doctrine and Covenants* reveals that, "They are Gods, even the Sons of God." (D & C 76:58) The Prophet Joseph Smith said:

> We have imagined and supposed that God was God from all eternity. I will refute the idea....God himself was once as we are now, and is an exalted man, and sits in yonder heavens....He was once a man like us; yea that God himself, the Father of us all, dwelt on an earth, the same as Jesus Christ himself did....
>
> Here then is eternal life—to know the only wise and true God; and you have to learn how to be Gods yourselves, and to be kings and priests to God, the same as all Gods have done before you, namely by going from one small degree to another, and from a small capacity to a great one; from grace to grace, from exaltation to exaltation, until you attain to the resurrection of the dead, and are able to dwell in everlasting burnings, and to sit in glory, as do those who sit enthroned in everlasting power. (*Teachings*, pp. 345-347; see also *Sermons*, p. 238)

This doctrine in no way detracts from the glory and power of the Heavenly Father. He will still remain the Father, and His children shall still be subject to Him. As they progress in glory and power their growth enhances and increases the glory and power of the Heavenly Father. According to Brigham Young: "The kingdoms he possesses and rules over are his own progeny. Every man who is faithful and gets a salvation and glory, becomes a King of Kings and Lord of Lords, or a Father of Fathers, it will be by the increase of his own progeny." (*Discourses of Young*, p. 25)

After all, what makes the Eternal Father a God? It is that which is under His dominion, His posterity and all the physical domain that He controls for His posterity to inhabit. The Lord said to John, "He that overcometh shall inherit all things; and I will be his God, and he will be my son." In speaking of the "sons" of God, the term includes the daughters also. Paul, writing to the Ephesian Saints said, "For this cause I bow my knee unto the Father of our Lord Jesus Christ, of whom the whole family in heaven and earth is named." (Ephesians 3:14-15) The family on earth is in *similitude* to the family in heaven: "And the same sociality which exists among us here will exist among us there, only it will be coupled with eternal glory, which glory we do not now enjoy." (D & C 130:2)

The Celestial Family Chain

Thus Godhood consists of an Eternal Father and Mother with their celestial family. The Father is patriarch over His family, and those of His worthy earthly sons who will become celestial patriarchs over their families, of which the patriarch of the families on earth is a *symbol*. These celestial family groups will be linked together in a patriarchal family chain. Elder Joseph Fielding Smith said: "Children born to parents who have obtained through their faithfulness, the fullness of these blessings shall be spirit children not clothed upon with tabernacles of flesh and bones. These children will be like we were before we came into this world." (*Doctrines of Salv.* Vol. 2, p. 68) Elder Orson Pratt said of them:

> Will not a man have his own family? Yes, he will also have his own mansion and farm, (*symbols* of whatever possessions a celestial being will have) his own sons and daughters. And what else? Why, the fact is man will continue to multiply and fill up his creation....

And what will he do when this is filled up? Why, he will make more worlds, and swarm out like bees from the old hive, and prepare new locations, and when a farmer has cultivated his farm and raised numerous children, so that the space is beginning to be too strait for them, he will say, "My sons, yonder is plenty of matter, go and organize a world, and people it, and you shall have laws to govern you, and you shall understand and comprehend through your experience the same things that we know. And thus it will be one eternal round, and one continual increase; and the government will be placed under those that are crowned as kings and priests in the presence of God." (*Discourses of Pratt*, p. 373)

The greatest happiness and joy in this life is achieved through family associations, and *similarly* the same will be true in the afterworld. Only those who attain the highest degree of the celestial kingdom will have the fullness of joy that will come through family ties and associations.

If a person can imagine all the good things of this life multiplied many times without pain, sorrow, or evil, then he can visualize in a small part what the celestial glory will be like. Paul said: "Eye hath not seen nor ear heard, neither have entered into the heart of man, the things which God hath prepared for them that love him." (1 Corinthians 2:9) Elder Melvin J. Ballard said:

What joy would it be merely to live, if one did not live with our loved ones? I am not so concerned where that place will be, and whether the streets shall be paved with gold and the walls set with diamond and jasper. I want it to be a place where I shall find my father, my mother, my brothers and sisters, my wife, and my children, my dear companions of this earth life. Give me them in a world like this, with sickness and death gone, and sin conquered, and it will be heaven enough for me. But give me streets paved with gold, and all the diamonds you can imagine and rob me of my loved ones and it would not be heaven to me. (*Sermons*, p. 189)

A Tangible Kingdom of Activity

The Latter-day Saint concept of the life anticipated in the Celestial Kingdom is one of activity, development and beauty. It will not be a dreamy, shadowy, immaterial existence, but a tangible, material reality.

It will be a *counterpart* of all the most desirable activities and things mankind enjoyed while on earth. The following description is from Elder Orson Pratt:

> A Saint who is one in deed and in truth, does not look for an immaterial heaven, but he expects a heaven with lands, houses, cities, vegetation, rivers and animals; with thrones, temples, palaces, kings, princes, priests and angels; with food, raiment, musical instruments etc., all of which are material. Indeed the Saint's heaven is a redeemed, glorified celestial material creation, inhabited by glorified material beings, male and female, organized into families, embracing all the relationships of husbands and wives, parents and children, where sorrow, crying, pain, and death will be no more. On it they expect to live with body, parts and holy passions; on it they expect to move and have being; to eat, drink, converse, worship, sing, play on musical instruments, engage in joyful innocent social amusements, visit neighboring towns and neighboring worlds. (*Discourses of Pratt*, p. 62)

Chapter 5

THE EARTH'S CREATION AND THE GARDEN OF EDEN

Spirits Chosen to Inhabit the Earth

Concerning the vastness of the universe, the scriptures deal primarily with eternal matters. As the millenniums of time passed, the Eternal Parents begat millions of spirit children in the premortal existence. Their spirit bodies and minds grew in stature and some developed more than others. God told Abraham that some of these spirits were more intelligent than others, that there were many "noble and great ones" and that "These will I make my rulers." (Abraham 3:19-23) His spirit children had reached a point in their eternal development where they could not develop further without mortal bodies and the experiences of mortal life, so He devised a plan of life and salvation to accomplish His eternal purposes. This plan included placing His spirit children on earth and sending His firstborn Son to live on earth and to act as a mediator, teacher and Savior for the rest of them. And God said, concerning a group of His spirit children:

> We will go down, for there is space there, and we will take of these materials, and we will make an earth whereon these may dwell: and we will prove them herewith to see if they will do all things whatsoever the Lord their God shall command them....
>
> And the Lord said: Whom shall I send? And one answered like unto the Son of Man: Here am I, send me. And another answered and said: Here am I send me. And the Lord said I will send the first. (Abraham 3:24-27)

The Father chose the first to be the Savior of the world because He accepted God's plan of life and salvation for mankind, but the other thought he should be the one to go although, He did not accept his Fathers plan. Since he was not selected, he rebelled and became Satan. (D & C 76:36-37)

> And I, the Lord God, spake unto Moses saying; That Satan...came before me, saying—Behold, here am I, send me, I will be thy son, and I will redeem all mankind, that not one soul shall be lost;...wherefore give me thine honor.
> But behold, my Beloved Son...said unto me—Father, thy will be done, and the glory be thine forever.
> Wherefore, because that Satan rebelled against me, and sought to destroy the agency of man, which I, the Lord God, had given him...I caused that he should be cast down,
> And he became Satan.... (Moses 4:1-4)

There were one third of the spirit children who turned away from the Father and followed Satan; these became the angels of the devil and were cast down to earth with him. (Revelations 12:9; D & C 29:37) The conflict between the Father and Satan was called by St. John a "war in heaven." Those who chose to follow Satan accepted his false doctrines and plan of salvation in the premortal life; *in like manner* those who believe the false doctrines and plan of salvation in this life are permitting themselves to be led away by Satan in the "war on earth." Satan attempted to destroy the free agency of the Father's children in the spirit world; *likewise*, he continues to try to do the same in man's mortal estate. Agency, the right to choose whether or not a person will keep or reject the commandments of God, is basic to all the principles and laws of God and the universe. It always has been and always will be.

We can understand more fully our life on earth if we visualize the close relationship between earth life and immortality. Joseph F. Smith said, "The things we experience here are *typical* of the things of God and the life beyond us. There is a great similarity between God's purposes as manifested here and his purposes as carried out in his presence and kingdom." (*Gospel Doctrine*, p. 462)

According to the Lord, the earthly creations of the Father are a *symbolic counterpart* of heavenly creations, and as such they *bear record* of Jesus Christ.

> ...and that all things may have their *likeness*, and that they may
> accord one with the other,...that which is earthly *conforming* to
> that which is heavenly. (D & C 128:12-13)

He has also revealed:

> All things have their *likeness*, and all things are created and
> made to *bear record* of me, both things which are temporal, and
> things which are spiritual; things which are in the heavens above
> and which are on the earth, and things which are in the earth
> and things which are under the earth, both above and beneath;
> all things *bear record* of me. (Moses 6:62-63)

The Lord revealed to the Prophet Joseph Smith that one is to
understand that the four beasts spoken of by John in Revelation 4:6
are symbols:

> They are *figurative* expressions, used by the Revelator John,
> in describing heaven, the Paradise of God, the happiness of man,
> and of beasts, and of creeping things, and of fowls of the air;
> that which is spiritual being in the *likeness* of that which is
> temporal; and that which is temporal is in the *likeness* of that
> which is spiritual; the spirit of man in the *likeness* of his person,
> as also the spirit of the beast, and every other creature which
> God has created...They...were shown to John to *represent* the glory
> of the classes of beings in their destined order or sphere of creation
> in the enjoyment of their eternal felicity. (D & C 77:2-4)

From the previous passage it is noted that not only man has a spirit
body but so also do other living creatures. The temporal bodies of all
living creatures are in the *likeness* or shape and form of their spiritual
bodies. Mankind is in the "express image of his (the Fathers) person;"
(Hebrews 1:3; Moses 6:9) The word image signifies the exact form
and shape of both the spiritual and mortal bodies. So far as one's mortal
body is normal, formed, and unimpaired by blemish, it is in the form
and shape of the spirit body which it tenants. "The spirit body shapes
the growing body of flesh and bone to resemble itself." (James E.
Talmage, *Vitality*, p. 243; *Saviors*, p. 5)

The Creation of the Earth and Those Who Dwell Thereon

Described in the books of Genesis, Moses, and Abraham are accounts of the creation of the earth and its inhabitants in six periods of time *symbolized* as six days. During the first "day" He formed light and divided the light from the darkness. On the second "day" He divided the waters from the firmament. On the third He caused the dry land to appear, the earth to bring forth grass, herbs, and trees. On the fourth He set the lights in the firmament, separating the day from the night. He made the stars also. On the fifth He created the fish of the sea and the fowl of the air each after their kind, and commanded them to multiply in the water and the earth. On the sixth he made the beasts of the earth and the cattle after their kind; and He created man in His own image, both male and female, and said for them to be fruitful and multiply and replenish the earth. (Genesis Chapter One) Chapter two of Genesis continues: "Thus the heavens and earth were finished, all host of them...and He rested on the seventh day from all His work." Verses four and five say that they were created, "every herb of the field before it grew; for the Lord God had not caused it to rain upon the earth, and there was not a man to till the ground." Then the chapter continues with an account of an earthly or physical creation of man, trees and beasts. The book of Moses adds:

> For I, the Lord God created all things, of which I have spoken, spiritually, before they were naturally upon the face of the earth...and I, the Lord God, had created all the children of men; and not yet a man to till the ground: for in heaven he created them...and I the Lord God formed man from the dust of the ground and breathed into his nostrils the breath of life; and man became a living soul, the first flesh upon the earth, the first man also, nevertheless, all things were before created; but spiritually were they created and made according to my word. (Moses 3:5-7)

Adam and Eve in the Garden of Eden

Thus the physical creation of the earth and all living things was in *similitude* of the spiritual creation that preceded it. The scriptures then proceed with a narrative of what transpired after the first man, Adam, was placed on earth:

> And I, the Lord God, took the man and put him into the Garden
> of Eden, to dress it, and to keep it.
>
> And I the Lord God commanded the man saying: Of every tree
> thou mayest freely eat,
>
> But of the tree of knowledge of good and evil, thou shall not
> eat of it, nevertheless, thou mayest choose for thyself for it is
> given unto thee; but remember that I forbid it for in the day thou
> eatest thereof thou shalt surely die.... (Moses 3:15-17)

Some individuals have suggested that the fruit of the tree of knowledge
of good and evil that Adam and Eve were forbidden to eat was *symbolic*
of a forbidden sex relationship. This assertion is untrue because they
were commanded by the Lord to multiply and replenish the earth,
(Genesis 1:28) necessitating a marriage relationship. Instead, the fruit
of the tree was *symbolic* of some particular law of the Garden and the
universe that by partaking of their own free agency would change them
and the earth from the immortal state they were in into a mortal state.
Adam, as head of the household in the Garden, was acting in *similitude*
of man's free agency and responsibility as head of the family on earth.
He was free to choose his course, and he was told that the consequences
of his decision would be death, which meant that he would be cut off
from the presence of God. *Likewise*, the Lord has told mankind through
the prophets that if they choose not to keep God's commandments,
they will, as did Adam, suffer the consequence which is spiritual death,
or being cast out from the presence of our Eternal Father throughout
eternity. The narrative continues:

> And I the Lord God said unto my only Begotten that it was
> not good that man shall be alone; wherefore I made an help meet
> for him....
>
> And I the Lord God, caused a deep sleep to fall upon Adam;
> and he slept, and I took one of his ribs and....
>
> Made I a woman, and brought her unto the man. (Moses 3:18,
> 21-22)

There has been much speculation about how Adam was created from
the dust of the earth and from which side of his body the rib was taken
in order to create Eve. In my opinion, the dust and rib are *symbolic
representations* of whatever natural eternal processes were utilized by
which Adam and Eve were placed on this earth. Adam's wife was called

"Eve" in *similitude* of her being the first mother of all women; (Moses 4:26) with the word "women" *representing* that she is part of man; and as man and wife that they would be as one flesh. (Genesis 2:23, 24)

Satan's Temptation of Eve

Some time after Adam and Eve were placed in the Garden of Eden, Satan attempted to deceive Adam, with the intent of thwarting the purposes of the Eternal Father concerning His plans for the world. Though Adam refused to accept His proposal, Satan was successful in tempting Eve. Following is a narrative of the account as recorded in the fourth chapter of the Book of Moses. The narrative in Genesis, Chapter 3, leaves out the verses which clarify that it was Satan who beguiled Eve through the mouth of the serpent. Nephi calls him "that old serpent, who is the devil." Thus the serpent is a *symbol* of Satan the devil. (2 Nephi 2:18)

Except as otherwise noted, the symbolic explanations that accompany the following quotations of the narrative are mine. The reader will better understand the symbolic representations of this narrative if he or she will relate it to the activities of mankind on earth with the serpent *representing* those people whom Satan uses to deceive and teach false doctrine to other people on earth. These people include anyone who teaches contrary to the revealed word of God.

> And now the serpent was more subtle than any beast of the field which I, the Lord God, had made.
>
> And Satan put it into the heart of the serpent, (for he had drawn away many after him,) (during premortality) and he sought also to beguile Eve, for he knew not the mind of God, wherefore he sought to destroy the world.
>
> And he said unto the woman; Yea, hath God said—Ye shall not eat of every tree of the garden? (And he spake by the mouth of the serpent.)
>
> And the woman said unto the serpent: We may eat of the fruit of the trees of the garden;
>
> But of the fruit of the tree which thou beholdest in the midst of the garden, God hath said—Ye shall not eat of it, neither shall ye touch it, lest ye die.
>
> And the serpent said unto the woman: Ye shall not surely die;

For God doth know that in the day ye eat thereof, then your eyes shall be opened, and ye shall be as the gods knowing good and evil.

The subtlety with which Satan deceived Eve, thereby using her to coerce Adam into a compromising situation is in *similitude* of the subtlety with which he uses half truths to deceive men and women on earth. The death of which God was speaking was spiritual as one is separated from His presence.

The Symbolic Counterparts Between the Garden and Mortality

"And when the woman saw that the tree was good for food, and that it became pleasant to the eyes, and the tree to be desired to make her wise, she took of the fruit thereof, and did eat, and also gave unto her husband with her, and he did eat." The steps and rationalization by which Eve yielded to the temptation of Satan and then influenced Adam into breaking God's commandment *symbolizes* the many ways in which people on earth rationalize and excuse themselves for breaking the commandments and then influence others to do likewise.

"And the eyes of them both were opened, and they knew that they had been naked. And they sewed fig leaves together and made themselves aprons." *Likewise* many people on earth, "by the power of the Spirit," have their eyes opened and their understandings "enlightened so as to understand the things of God." (D & C 76:12-13) The act of making fig leaf aprons to cover their nakedness could be in *similitude* to the actions men and women take in order to cover up or correct the mistakes and wrong doings they made while unenlightened.

"And they heard the voice of the Lord God, as they were walking in the garden; and Adam and his wife went to hide themselves from the presence of the Lord God amongst the trees of the garden." *Likewise* many people on earth try to hide themselves from the presence of the Lord and His church representatives on earth after they realize they have broken commandments of the Lord.

"And I, the Lord God, called unto Adam, and said unto him; Where goest thou? And he said: I heard thy voice in the garden, and I was afraid, because I beheld that I was naked, and I hid myself." *Similarly*, fear of the Lord or his representatives, coupled with shame, causes many members of the church, after they have broken commandments, to hide themselves by becoming inactive and staying away from church.

> And I, the Lord God, said unto Adam: Who told thee thou wast naked? Hast thou eaten of the tree whereof I commanded thee that thou shouldst not eat, if so thou shouldst surely die?
>
> And the man said: The woman thou gavest me, and commandest that she should remain with me, she gave me of the fruit of the tree and I did eat.
>
> And I, the Lord God, said unto the woman: What is this thing which thou hast done? And the woman said: The serpent beguiled me and I did eat.

Similarly, those who become inactive find many excuses for their inactivity, blaming what church members and others do and say.

> And I, the Lord God, said unto the serpent: Because thou hast done this thou shalt be cursed above all the cattle, and above every beast of the field; upon thy belly shalt thou go, and dust shalt thou eat all the days of thy life;
>
> And I will put emnity between thee and the woman, between thy seed and her seed; and he shall bruise thy head, and thou shalt bruise his heel.

Satan was given great power to tempt and cause distress for the descendants of Adam and Eve; but the foregoing passages *symbolically* illustrate the greater power given to mankind to overcome Satan's influence. While speaking to the Seventy about their power over Satan, the Lord said: "Behold I give unto you power to tread on serpents and scorpions and over all power of the enemy." (Luke 10:17-19)

Adam and Eve Chastized and the Earth Cursed

> Unto the woman, I, the Lord God, said: I will greatly multiply thy sorrow and thy conception. In sorrow thou shalt bring forth children, and thy desire shall be to thy husband, and he shall rule over thee.
>
> And Unto Adam, I, the Lord God, said: Because thou hast hearkened unto the voice of thy wife, and hast eaten of the fruit of the tree of which I commanded thee, saying—Thou shalt not

eat of it, cursed shall be the ground for thy sake; in sorrow shalt
thou eat of it all the days of thy life.

Thorns, also, and thistles shall it bring forth to thee, and thou
shalt eat the herb of the field.

By the sweat of thy face shalt thou eat bread, until thou shalt
return unto the ground—for thou shalt surely die—for out of it
was thou taken: for dust thou wast, and unto dust shalt thou return.

The sorrow, cursed ground, thorns, thistles, sweat of the face and
descriptions concerning them are *symbolic* of the struggle in the lives
of men and women during life on earth as they prepare themselves
to meet the Lord after completing their earth life.

"And Adam called his wife's name Eve, because she was the mother
of all living....Unto Adam, and also unto his wife, did I, the Lord God,
make coats of skins, and clothed them." The coats of skins *represent*
that men and women should be amply clothed at all times. Nephi *likens*
nakedness to unrighteousness while "being clothed with purity yea,
even with the robe of righteousness" *symbolizes* righteous actions. (2
Nephi 9:14)

Adam and Eve Cast Out of Eden

And I, the Lord God, said unto mine Only Begotten: Behold,
the man is become as one of us to know good and evil; and now
lest he put forth his hand and partake also of the tree of life, and
live forever,

Therefore, I, the Lord God, will send him forth from the garden
of Eden, to till the ground from whence he was taken;...

So I drove out the man, and I placed at the east of the   garden
of Eden, Cherubim and a flaming sword, which turned every way
to keep the way of the tree of life. (Moses 4:1-31; Genesis   3:1-24)

While the tree of knowledge of good and evil *represented* mankind's
activities and attainments during his sojourn on earth, the tree of life
is *symbolic* of the love of God and spiritual or eternal life that we may
attain after resurrection. (1 Nephi 11:22, 25) After Adam partook of
the tree of knowledge of good and evil, it was imperative that he,
representing mankind, did not partake of any portion of the tree of
life without first meeting certain requirements. These requirements are

explained in later chapters of this book, and all must be met in order for a person to obtain a fullness of eternal life.

Adam and Eve were cast out of the Garden of Eden so that they could not eat of the tree of life, which would have caused them to live forever in the pre-mortal state they were in. To further insure against their doing so, the Lord placed Cherubim (plural of Cherub) and a flaming sword in order that they should not partake of the fruit thereof. (Alma 42:3) The reason they were not permitted to partake was that the Garden of Eden was still part of the pre-mortal state of man, and without the fall Adam and Eve would forever have remained in that state; a state in which they never would have had any posterity. Thus they nor anyone else would have attained exaltation. The prophet Lehi said:

> If Adam had not transgressed he would not have fallen, but he would have remained in the Garden of Eden. And all things which were created must have remained in the same state in which they were after they were created; and they must have remained forever, and had no end.
>
> And they would have had no children; wherefore, they would have remained in a state of innocence, having no joy, for they knew no misery; doing no good for they knew no sin. (2 Nephi 2:22-23; see also Moses 5:11)

The original plan of the Father was not frustrated nor defeated. Instead, the fall was all part of an elaborate and glorious plan of the Eternal Father, whereby man could become mortal and learn from the earthlife *counterpart* of the "tree of knowledge of good and evil." When Satan said to Eve "that in the day ye eat thereof, then your eyes shall be opened; and ye shall be as the Gods; knowing good and evil," he was speaking the truth. She did eat, her eyes were opened and she learned good and evil. *Likewise* men and women must open their eyes in order to become as God. They must experience the good and evil influences that came into the world as the earth fell during Adam's expulsion from the Garden, and they must live correct principles. The tree of life and the contrasting forbidden fruit are in *similitude* of man's learning from the bitter in contrast to the sweet, and also of learning from the good in contrast to learning evil, "for it must be that there is an opposition in all things." (2 Nephi 2:11-15, Moses 6:55)

Satan's Influence Continues

Satan and his followers have not given up; they are still fighting their war of deceit and evil. As they were cast out of heaven, they were cast down to earth. (Rev. 12:9; Luke 10:17-18) The Lord revealed that "he became Satan, yea the devil, the father of all lies, to deceive and to blind men, and to lead them captive at his will, even as many as would not harken to my voice." (Moses 4:4) However, the evil designs of Satan serve the Lord's purpose in His eternal plan of life and salvation, in that man learns to develop good qualities and capabilities by overcoming evil influences.

As a result of the fall, Adam was cast out of the Garden of Eden from the Father's presence. *Likewise*, all of God's spirit children (other than those who followed Satan) undergo a spiritual separation from the Eternal Father when they are born into mortal life. These spirit children were not in the Garden, nor did they individually partake of the forbidden fruit that caused the spiritual death of Adam and Eve, but the fall of all mankind was *represented* by the fall of Adam, From then on, all dealings of the Father or the Son with Adam became a *symbol* of the Lord with all of Adam's descendants, He being the father of mankind on earth. They are expected to do all that the Lord expected of Adam the same as if they are Adam.

Chapter Six

POINTING TOWARDS CHRIST'S ATONEMENT

Christ Chosen as Savior

In the ante-mortal existence, ages before the Father cast Satan to the earth and before He permitted Satan to tempt Adam, He planned a means whereby the fall of man would be surmounted. Christ "was foreordained before the foundations of the world" (1 Peter 1:20, Moses 4:2) for that purpose. Jesus Christ was chosen and sent by His Eternal Father to come to earth and act as the savior of mankind and thus atone for the fall of Adam. This atonement made it possible that everyone who comes to earth will be redeemed from the death caused by the fall of Adam, and all will be resurrected. "For as in Adam all die, even so in Christ shall all be made alive." (1 Corinthians 15:22)

The atonement comes to all mankind from the time of the fall of Adam "even unto the end of the world." (Mosiah 4:7) It is unconditional insofar as redeeming man from the physical death; all men will be resurrected as a free gift from Jesus Christ. Christ will eventually subdue all things, "even to the destroying of Satan and his works, at the end of the world, and the last great day of judgment." (D & C 19:2-3)

Adam and Eve Begin Mortal Life

After Adam and Eve were cast out of the Garden, they began to labor and till the earth. They also began to bear sons and daughters. Their sons and daughters divided two by two, tilled the land and tended the flocks, and they in turn begat sons and daughters. And Adam and Eve, his wife, called upon the name of the Lord,

And he gave unto them commandments, that they should worship the Lord their God, and should offer the firstlings of their flocks, for an offering unto the Lord. And Adam was obedient unto the commandments of the Lord.

And after many days an angel of the Lord appeared unto Adam, saying: Why dost thou offer sacrifices unto the Lord? And Adam said unto him: I know not, save the Lord commanded me.

And then the angel spake, saying: This thing is in *similitude* of the sacrifice of the Only Begotten of the Father, which is full of grace and truth.

Wherefore, thou shalt do all that thou doest in the name of the Son, and thou shalt repent and call upon God in the name of the Son forevermore. (Moses 5:5-8)

Sacrifices as Symbols of Christ and His Life

Adam was commanded to offer up sacrifices to the Lord which the angel said was "in *similitude* of the sacrifice of the Only Begotten." From the beginning, the offerings were prescribed in a set manner so as to properly *symbolize* the future atonement of Christ. The offerings of Cain, a son of Adam, were not acceptable because they were of "the fruit of the ground," but Abel "brought of the firstlings of his flock, and of the fat thereof. And the Lord had respect unto Abel and to his offering." (Genesis 4:1-4) Not only was an animal required in order to *represent* the body of Christ, but the sacrifice was to be a *symbol* of his very life. The "firstlings of the flock" was in *similitude* of him as the firstborn of the Father, and the fat thereof *represented* Him as the very best. Although Cain was a farmer, if he had possessed the proper attitude he would have raised, or otherwise secured, the correct offering—one *symbolic* of the proper attitude that man should have toward all the commandments of God. In order for the activities of men and women to be accepted by the Lord they must obey the principles and commandments of the gospel as prescribed by the Lord and not change them to suit their own ideas and desires.

At the time the Israelites were to be delivered from bondage in Egypt, the Lord commanded that they should take the blood from lambs and goats and strike it on the door posts of the houses, "And the blood shall be to you for a *token*...and when I see the blood, I will pass over you...And this day shall be a *memorial*....That ye shall say, it is the sacrifice of the Lord's passover...." (Exodus 12:13-14, 27) The placing of blood on the door posts *represented* obedience, for which blessings were promised. The lamb to be sacrificed had to be of the first year, (Exodus 12:5) without blemish and without spot (1 Peter 1:19) as a *symbol* of Christ's perfect life; and "neither shall ye break a bone thereof..." (Exodus 12:46; Psalms 34:20) as a *sign* that none of Christ's bones were to be broken during his crucifixion. (John 19:33-36)

Each year after the Israelites were delivered from bondage, they were commanded to observe the ordinance of the passover as an *emblem* that Christ would come to earth and deliver them and all of mankind from the bonds of death. The blood spilled upon the altar was a *symbol* of the blood of Christ that was to be spilled: "For the life of the flesh is in the blood; and I have given it to you upon the altar to make an atonement for your souls; for it is in the blood that maketh an atonement for the soul." (Leviticus 17:11; Revelation 1:5) Thus, the blood of the sacrifice of the passover and of Jesus Christ was a *symbol* of both the giving of one's life and of the receiving of immortal life through the atonement.

As an extreme test of faith, the Lord commanded Abraham to offer his son Isaac as a burnt offering on the altar, but when Abraham and Isaac demonstrated their willingness to obey, an angel of the Lord stopped him and replaced Isaac with a ram for the sacrifice. While recalling this event the prophet Jacob said that the Israelites kept the laws of sacrifice because it pointed their souls to Christ: "And for this cause it is sanctified unto us for righteousness even as it was accounted unto Abraham, to be obedient unto the commands of God in offering up his son Isaac, which is a *similitude* of God and his Only Begotten Son." (Jacob 4:5) Inasmuch as the sacrifice of Isaac was never completed, it was a *symbol* only to teach the Israelites of the magnitude of the future sacrifice of the Savior. Although Isaac's birth was not as miraculous as that of Jesus, his birth to Sarah was foretold *in similitude* to that of Jesus's birth to Mary. (Genesis 17:15-19)

As a "father of many nations," Abraham appropriately *represented* the Eternal Father of Jesus. Paul called Isaac "the only begotten son," (Hebrews 11:17) the same as was Christ. Historians have determined that Isaac, at the time of Abraham's offering, was about the same age as Jesus was at the time of his crucifixion. Isaac went to the altar willingly in *similitude* to Jesus's willing acceptance of the will of His

Eternal Father. (Matthew 26:39) Christ was obedient to the eternal laws of God and the universe when he was crucified. *Likewise*, the *symbolic* obedience in "the sacrifice required of Abraham in the offering up of Isaac shows that if a man would attain to the keys of the kingdom of an endless life he must sacrifice all things." (*Teachings*, p. 322) Such keys are required for a person to attain exaltation, which is eternal life.

Symbolic Sacrifices Many and Varied

As with many other commandments under Moses, the law of sacrifice became varied and complex, with a multitude of rules established to govern the procedures. Among the different types of sacrifices were "burnt offerings," *symbolically* named from the idea of the smoke of the sacrifice ascending to heaven, while the act *symbolized* the consecration of the worshiper to Jehovah. A "sin offering" was *representative* of the people, and a "peace offering" an *indication* that the sacrificer was at peace with God. When all three types were offered at the same time, "the sin preceded the burnt, and the burnt, the peace offerings. Thus the order of the *symbolizing* sacrifices were the order of the atonement, sanctification, and fellowship with the Lord." (*LDS Bible Dictionary:* "Sacrifices")   Because Christ is the cornerstone of the gospel and of the kingdom of God, everything righteous is in *similitude* of Him and His atoning sacrifice, "and all things which have been given of God from the beginning of the world unto man, are the *typifying* of him." (2 Nephi 11:4) Christ said,"all things have their *likeness*, and all things are created and made to *bear record* of me..." (Moses 6:63) Amulek added, "This is the whole meaning of the law, every whit pointing to that great and last sacrifice; and that great and last sacrifice will be the Son of God." (Alma 34:14)

One of the early symbols came when the Israelites were complaining against Moses and against God. Because of their complaints the Lord "sent fiery serpents among the people, and they bit the people; and much people died." The people came to Moses and asked him to pray in their behalf. According to the Lord's instructions, "Moses made a serpent of brass and put it upon a pole, and it came to pass, that if a serpent had bitten any man, when he beheld the serpent of brass, he lived." (Numbers 21:5-9) Alma indicated that this procedure was *typifying* the Lord in that "a *type* was raised up in the wilderness, that whosoever would look upon it might live." (Alma 33:19) Nephi, while prophesying concerning the coming of the son of God, said that as Moses

> ...lifted up the brazen serpent in the wilderness *even so* shall he be lifted up who should come.
>
> And as many as should look upon that serpent should live, *even so* as many should look upon the Son of God with faith, having a contrite spirit, might live, even unto that life which is eternal. (Helaman 8:13-15)

As is recorded in John, Christ said, "And as Moses lifted up the serpent in the wilderness *even so* must the Son of Man be lifted up: That whosoever believeth in him should not perish but have everlasting life." (John 3:14-15)

Here Christ adds that one who is to receive eternal life must believe in Him. In John 3:5, Christ states that "except a man be born of the water and of the spirit he cannot enter the kingdom of the Lord." Thus the faith and contrite spirit required in order for a person to be healed as he obediently looked at the brazen serpent was in *similitude* of the belief and faith that is required of a person as he contritely and obediently submits to the baptism of the water and the spirit.

The Serpent Also a Symbol of Christ

Just as the serpent can *symbolize* Christ and eternity in the highest sense, it is, also, used to *represent* Satan and the lowest forms of life. Snake, serpent and viper are words *denoting* a reptile that crawls on the ground. In the scriptures a serpent or viper is *symbolic* of a subtle, evil and treacherous person or the Devil. (Dictionaries; Matthew 3:7; D & C 76:28-31; Revelation 12:9) Christ called the Pharisees, Sadducees, and others a generation of serpents and vipers because of their deceitful methods (Matthew 3:7; 12:34; 23:83) Of them He said, "Wo unto all those that discomfort my people, and drive, and murder, and testify against them, saith the Lord of Hosts; a generation of vipers shall not escape the damnation of Hell." (D & C 121:23) Therefore, as one must keep the Tree of Life and the Tree of Knowledge of Good and Evil in correct focus, so must he seek to be certain that whatever seems on the surface to come from the Lord of a surety does, for Satan often twists the truth to suit his needs. Job had this in mind when he said that "the viper's tongue shall slay him (mankind)." (Job 20:16)

This principle was very aptly illustrated when Lucifer tempted Eve through the mouth of the serpent, by telling her she should not surely die but that her eyes would be opened and she would be as the gods knowing good and evil. He only told part truths and thus the serpent became a *symbol* of deception, evil, destruction and death. (*Life Symbols,* p. 137) As it crawls on its belly on the ground, the serpent is a *symbol* of Satan having been cast out of the presence of God into darkness, as will be the lot of those who follow him. Conversely, Christ being lifted up on the cross is a *symbol* of light and life unto all those who follow him. Christ *likened* his being lifted up on the cross as to what was expected of all men:

> And my Father sent me that I might be lifted up upon the cross;...and after that I had been lifted up on the cross, that I might draw all men unto me that as I have been lifted up by men even so should men be lifted up by the Father, to stand before me, and to be judged of their works, whether they be good or whether they be evil. (3 Nephi 27:14-15)

> Although no present-day statue of Christ's crucifixion is to be worshiped, to any degree, one can look at them, and at pictures of the Lord, and be reminded of the nails that pierced his hands, wrists and feet. And "We see the gash in his pierced side from whence came the blood and water as a *sign* that the atonement had been wrought." (Bruce R. McConkie, *Ensign*, June 1982, p. 15)

Christ and His Atoning Sacrifice

In a mortal state, Adam and Even and all their posterity were powerless to be resurrected and to enter into kingdoms of glory, but Christ possessed this power within Himself. Though He lived on earth as other men, yet He was innately different. Though He was born of Mary, a mortal mother, He was begotten in the flesh by an immortal Father in heaven. With this combination of mortality and Godhood He had both the capacity to die and also the power to control life, death and resurrection. Having thus been born with these rights and powers, as one of the Godhead, He is the First Begotten of the Father in the flesh.

Possessing attributes of both Godhood and manhood, He was able to live in a world of sin and corruption, become tempted by Satan, yet live a life pure and sinless. He was able to atone for the sins of the world and redeem mankind by means of His crucifixion and resurrection. It was necessary for the one undertaking this mission to be perfect, without sin or blemish. Christ was the only being worthy of such a sacrifice. It is doubtful that anyone fully understands the deep meaning and purpose of the Atonement of Christ and how it operates, yet it is a foundation of the Gospel of Jesus Christ. He "died, was buried, and rose again the third day, and ascended to heaven; and all other things that pertain to our religion are only apendages to it." (*Teachings*, p. 121) Therefore such apendages as birth, baptism, death, and resurrection point *symbolically* to Jesus Christ.

The atonement consists of a process under which Christ overcame and nullified both the temporal and spiritual death of mankind brought about by the fall of Adam and Eve. He overcame the temporal death unconditionally, while overcoming spiritual death is conditioned upon the actions of each individual during mortality. Through the free gift of Christ's atonement on the cross, everyone is given immortality as a gift, without works of righteousness being required. On the other hand, eternal life and all other spiritual rewards are given in proportion to obedience to the requirements of the laws prescribed and governed by God. When Christ atoned for the fall of Adam, he appeased and made amends for the penalty of death. He reconciled man to God (Jacob 4:11) by means of a ransom and redemption (Isaiah 35:9-10). Because of Christ's atonement man, by his own acts of obedience to law, may be brought from a state of evil and spiritual darkness and be restored to a state of sanctity with our Eternal Father. Amulek bore this testimony of the atonement:

> I do know that Christ shall come among the children of men to take upon him the transgressions of his people, and he shall atone for the sins of the world....
>
> For according to the plan of the Eternal God there must be an atonement made, or else mankind must unavoidably perish....
>
> For it is expedient that there should be a great and last sacrifice; yea, not a sacrifice of man, neither of beast, neither of any manner of fowl; for it shall not be a human sacrifice; but it must be an infinite and eternal sacrifice.
>
> Now there is not any man that can sacrifice blood which will atone for the sins of another....(Alma 34:8-12)

Man cannot sacrifice his own blood for another person, nor can he sacrifice his own blood in order to atone for his own sins. But the sacrifice of the time and means that one makes as he or she helps other people while serving in church positions, *symbolically represents* Christ's atoning sacrifice. As "mankind should unavoidably perish," without the atonement of Christ, *likewise* men and women shall perish insofar as celestial glory is concerned without their service in God's kingdom on earth. The *symbolism* of service is especially true when a person labors in genealogical and temple activities.

Chapter Seven

PROBATION IN THE PHYSICAL WORLD

The Plan of Salvation

There are two basic rewards of Christ's atonement. First, there is a general salvation for all mankind, exempting them from the permanent effects of the fall of Adam insofar as mortal death is concerned. The second is for an individual to receive a personal salvation through a remission of sins and the development of his powers and capabilities. With the second reward comes the power that can enable every individual to throw off the effects of Satan completely and to become pure and perfect as Christ. He ultimately may receive the power to become a son or daughter of God as a joint-heir with Christ in the Celestial Kingdom. (D & C 39:6; Romans 8:14-17)

Ages before Adam was placed in the Garden, the Eternal Father devised the Plan of Salvation whereby achieving the second reward can be accomplished. As He prepared to send his spirit children to dwell on earth He said:

> We will prove them herewith, to see if they will do all things whatsoever the Lord their God shall command them;
>
> And they who keep their first estate shall be added upon; and they who keep not their first estate shall not have glory in the same kingdom with those who keep their first estate; and they who keep their second estate shall have glory added upon their heads forever and ever. (Abraham 3:25-26)

The "first estate" is the period of pre-mortal life wherein all the spirits were born and lived as spirit children of the Eternal Mother and Father. Those who kept their first estate are those who accepted the Father's plan of life and salvation in the premortal life and are thereby permitted to dwell on earth. Those who rejected His plan did not keep their first estate and were therefore not permitted to dwell on earth. The "second estate" is man's probation during his lifetime on earth. The Eternal Father has given all his spirit children who did not follow Satan the opportunity to come to earth and obtain earthly bodies. Here they may gain the additional experience and training necessary to prove themselves worthy and capable of becoming sons and daughters of God. As He said:

> And I give unto you a commandment, that ye shall forsake all evil and cleave unto all good, that ye shall live by every word which proceedeth forth out of the mouth of God;
> For he will give unto the faithful line upon line, precept upon precept; and I will try you and prove you herewith...in all things, whether you will abide in my covenant, even unto death, that you may be found worthy; (D & C 98:11-15)

He also said,

> My people must be tried in all things, that they may be prepared to receive the glory that I have in store for them. (D & C 136:31)

Of course, in order for one to prove himself, he must do it of his own free will and choice. Free-agency is guaranteed in mortal life the *same as* it is while men are unembodied spirits. Satan's plan to put mankind on earth and to force all to obey God's commandments would not prove anyone worthy of the highest glory. A person may be forced to do many things, but he does not develop his capabilities of leadership and self motivation from forced experiences. He would be nothing more than a mere subject; he would not be capable of an heirship in the kingdom of heaven.

Man Can Become as God

Many people think that free agency signifies that they have the right to do as they please without anyone, including God, commanding or dictating what they should or should not do. Usually their rights, as they suppose, are based without regard to the consequences of their actions or whom they may affect or injure. Agency is man's right to choose between opposites, with the expectation that he will reap the consequences of his choices whether they are for better or for worse. As was the case with Adam and Eve, men and women are given the right to choose for themselves whether or not to obey the commandments or God; and as with them, the Father has prescribed the consequences: "Wherefore men are free according to the flesh...and they are free to choose liberty and eternal life through the great mediator of all men, or to choose the captivity and power of the devil." (2 Nephi 2:27)

When God commanded Adam not to eat of the tree of knowledge of good and evil, he emphasized the eternal principle of freedom to choose, but also of the consequences, saying "thou mayest choose for thyself, for it is given unto thee; but, remember that I forbid it, for in the day thou takest thereof thou shalt surely die." (Moses 3:17) *Likewise* all who choose to break God's commandments during their life on earth will die spiritually. Thus, those who think they are choosing the road to freedom when they rebel against God's commandments are losing their freedom and coming under "the power and captivity of Satan, he having subjected them according to his will." (Alma 12:17) In contrast, those who accept and obey God's commandments prove themselves worthy and capable of attaining the greatest freedom of all, a partial freedom from the power of Satan in this life, which is a *counterpart* of the complete freedom to be enjoyed as sons and daughters of the Eternal Father in His eternal kingdom.

With true freedom man also realizes the Latter-day Saint interpretation of the word "joy." Lehi said to his son Jacob, "Adam fell that man might be; and men are that they might have joy." (2 Nephi 2:25) A fullness of joy does not come until one attains exaltation; "for in this world your joy is not full, but in me your joy is full." (D & C 101:36) Joy should not be confused with pleasure. Pleasures result from everyday activities, including many that are unrighteous. A measure of joy is enjoyed by those in this life who live as closely as they are able to the commandments of the Lord, which joy is in *similitude* to the fullness of joy of those who will become sons and daughters of God.

In the post-mortal life no one is going to have a fullness of joy unless he continues to create. Those who are otherwise intelligent people but refuse to obey the full Gospel of Jesus Christ are going to be disappointed because they will be denied creative powers. The full creative powers of the universe will belong to those who attain exaltation, those who will continue to expand and develop until they become as God now is, those who will have millions of spirit children and then create worlds and systems of worlds for them to inhabit. Elder Orson Pratt said:

> Then we shall know, by experience, how to appreciate as well as to distinguish between happiness and misery, and be as the Gods, knowing good and evil. Is this lesson necessary? Yes, suppose the Lord were to appoint to you a kingdom; suppose he were to say to you: 'Son, yonder are materials which you may organize by my power into a world; you may place upon it your own offspring, as I did my offspring upon the world upon which you dwell.' What kind of a person would you be if you had no experience? What? Go and create a world, and then people that world with your own offspring, and not know the difference between good and evil, between sickness and health, between pain and happiness, having no knowledge of these by experience. I think that such a one would not be fitted to be entrusted with a world that was to undergo and pass through the same ordeals that our creation is now experiencing. (*Discourses of Pratt*, p. 302)

All that one does in righteousness represents some necessary experience on his climb upward and each of these experiences is *symbolic* of something that the Eternal Father does, which man in turn must learn to do. Brigham Young said:

> We organize according to men in the flesh by combining the elements and planting the seed, we cause vegetables, trees, grains, etc., to come forth. We are organizing a kingdom here according to the pattern that the Lord has given for people in the flesh, but not for those who have resurrection, although it is a *similitude*. (*Discourses of Young*, p. 398)

The Priesthood on Earth and in Heaven

The power by which all things are organized and controlled is called the Priesthood. The priesthood of the universe held by the Eternal Father is of a much higher order than its symbolic counterpart that is held by men on earth, the earthly priesthood, Parley P. Pratt said:

And moreover, the Lord has appointed a Holy Priesthood on the earth and in the heavens, and also in the world of spirits, which priesthood is after the order or *similitude* of His Son. (*Journal*, Vol. 2, p. 45)

John Taylor also said,

It is the government of God, whether on earth or in the heavens; for it is by that power, agency or principle that all things are governed on earth and in the heavens.(John Taylor, *Millennial Star*, Vol. 9, Nov. 1, 1849)

And Joseph F. Smith taught that the priesthood is

That authority which God has delegated to man, by which men are empowered to bind on earth and it shall be bound in heaven...(*Gospel Doctrine*, p. 174)

In the priesthood on earth there are two main divisions. The greater, or Melchizedek, was formerly called the "Holy Priesthood, after the Order of the Son of God...and has power and authority over all offices in the church in all ages of the world to administer in spiritual things." (D & C 107:2-8) The lesser priesthood, called the Priesthood of Aaron, has the power and authority to administer in temporal matters and ordinances and is an appendage of the Melchizedek Priesthood. (D & C 107:13-14)

While Jesus Christ was on earth, He ministered through the authority of the priesthood He held, using it in both spiritual and material matters. *Likewise*, by the authority of the priesthood man holds, he administers in the spiritual and temporal activities of The Church of Jesus Christ of Latter-day Saints. Within the priesthood organization are many offices to which men (and women in auxiliary organizations) are called to serve. Indirectly, these offices *represent* activities in the celestial glory. Through the functioning of the members in these offices, they gain the experience necessary to prepare themselves to be worthy and capable of the activities of the Father's kingdom.

In the organization of the priesthood there are six basic quorums. Worthy boys are normally called to be deacons at age twelve. They are primarily assistants to the teachers, priests and men holding the Melchizedek Priesthood. The Teacher's duty is to "watch over the church always, and be with and strengthen them." Deacons and Teachers

may be assigned to pass the sacrament, to collect fast offerings, and
to fulfill other assignments under the direction of the Bishop. It is the
Priest's duty to preach, teach, baptize and administer to the Sacrament.
He also has authority to ordain priests, teachers and deacons.

In addition to holding all the powers and responsibilities of the
Aaronic Priesthood, an Elder also is authorized to confirm those who
are baptized, to administer to the sick and to conduct meetings. High
Priests have the right to officiate and to administer in spiritual as well
as material things. The primary responsibility of the Seventies is to
carry the Gospel to the world. (*Priesthood Government*, pp. 115-116;
D & C Sections 70 and 107)

Each of the local groups of quorums has a president (or leader) and
two counselors. These are *counterparts* of the presidency of the Church
and Kingdom of God on earth and in heaven. These positions give
leadership experience to those in office. The Secretarial positions
represent the vast system of records that must be kept in heaven. A
bishop supervises a local group of members called a ward, which is
similar to a parish or congregation of other churches except that the
bishop receives no money for his services. Throughout the wards and
stakes, those called to service in the priesthood, Sunday School, Relief
Society, youth organizations, welfare and other organizations do so
without any remuneration, as part of God's way of giving everyone
all the experience possible for them to become capable and worthy
of their future *counterpart*, the eternal government of the heavens.

The Sustaining of Proper Authority

As members are called into their church position, they must be
sustained by the members of the particular group or organization to
which they are called. (D & C 20:65) There is an important lesson
to be learned concerning *symbolic representation* as members sustain
an individual to a particular position. They raise their right hand and
represent that they will support the one called in his position; that they
support and sustain those who called them; that they sustain the prophet
of the Church; and that they support and sustain the Father, the Son
and the Holy Ghost who inspired that calling. Thus to whatever extent
man supports and sustains those called, including his own position,
by his actions, it is *symbolic* of the support and obedience he is preparing
himself to give to God the Father in the postmortal life.

The entire organization of The Church of Jesus Christ of Latter-day Saints *represents* the perfect order of the priesthood that is necessary to control the universe. In the heavens there can be no confusion or disorder. If there were any confusion and antagonism between those controlling the systems of planets and stars they would destroy each other. Anyone who attains celestial glory first must learn his place in the priesthood organization and learn to whom he is responsible, in order to know his future responsibilities in the universe and to whom he will be responsible.

The Church of Jesus Christ is organized as nearly perfectly as possible in order for the members to experience and learn the proper order and chain of authority. Jesus Christ is at the head of the Church with a Prophet selected to represent Him here on earth. He, under authority of Christ, delegates all activities through his apostles, stake and ward organizations, regional representatives and others. Each office has a definitely prescribed chain of authority with all its attending duties. Any confusion comes because of man's imperfections while he is attempting to reach perfection.

President Joseph F. Smith said:

> Every man ordained to any degree of the priesthood has the authority delegated to him. But it is necessary that every act performed under this authority shall be done at the proper time and place and in the proper way, and after the proper order. The power of directing these labors constitutes the keys of the priesthood. (*Gospel Doctrine*, p. 168; Amos 3:7)

These keys are in *similitude* of the keys of authority that are directing the powers that are controlling the universe. It is important for those who hold such keys or who are in positions of authority to learn not to exercise improper authority in the positions in which they officiate; otherwise they will be incapable of governing as sons of the Father in the universe.

While on earth Christ served as the Mediator between the Father and mankind. (Hebrews 9:15; D & C 76:69) In a *similar* manner, man, holding church positions of authority, is a mediator between the Lord and those he serves, as were the priests and Moses in Old Testament times, who served "unto the *example* and *shadow* of heavenly things." (Hebrew 8:1-6)

Chapter Eight

THE FIRST PRINCIPLES AND ORDINANCES OF THE GOSPEL

Faith and Repentance

Encompassed within the priesthood of the universe are many principles and ordinances necessary for individual exaltation, the first of which are: faith, repentance, baptism and the laying on of hands for the gift of the Holy Ghost.

Faith is the first step on the ladder to exaltation. No one could have confidence enough to establish and control a universe if he did not develop faith to do it; and learning to have faith without exact knowledge is the Lord's way of teaching confidence. Moroni said: "I would show the world that faith is things which are hoped for and not seen." (Ether 12:6) Faith is that conviction within a person that causes him to act and do things. A farmer may believe that crops will grow, but if he lets doubts and fears of drought, frost, weeds, and disease take away his faith in a good harvest, he will not plant. *Likewise* if a person does not develop enough faith and confidence to construct and people a world, he will never do it.

One would think there would be no need for repentance in heaven as there would be no sin, but sin is the disobeying or breaking of God's laws and commandments. Satan and his followers sinned when they rebelled in the premortal existence. It is probable that there was a provision in the Father's plan for them to repent, but they chose not to do so. The strength and understanding man gains from his experience with repentance on earth will enable him to better understand the repentance he will require of his offspring, if and when he attains eternal life and places them in a future mortal existence.

Baptism as the Gateway

The third principle and the first essential ordinance of the gospel is baptism, the gateway into the Church of Jesus Christ, the kingdom of God on earth and its *symbolic* counterpart, the kingdom of heaven. There can be no membership in God's kingdom on earth without baptism by those delegated of God to perform such ordinances. *Likewise* without entrance into His earthly kingdom, there can be no entrance into the celestial kingdom:

> Verily, verily, I say unto you, they who believe not on your words, and are not baptized in water in my name for the remission of sins, that they may receive the Holy Ghost, shall be damned, and shall not come into my Father's kingdom where my Father and I am. (D & C 84:74)

The exact method of baptism is prescribed by the Lord: The one officiating "shall go down into the water with the person....Then shall he immerse him or her in the water, and come forth out of the water." (D & C 20:73-74) After which those holding the Melchizedek priesthood lay their hands on the person and bestow the Holy Ghost upon him. With this act he is also confirmed a member of Christ's church. (Acts 8:14-20; D & C 20:41)

Baptism as a Complex Symbol

Baptism is one of the most symbolic of all ordinances of the gospel. Foremost it is a *representation* to Jesus Christ "as a witness before him that ye have entered into a covenant with him, that ye will serve him and keep his commandments...." (Mosiah 18:10) Paul said:

> Therefore we are buried with him by baptism unto death: that *like as* Christ was raised up from the dead by the glory of the Father, *even so* we also should walk in newness of life.
>
> For if we have been planted together in the *likeness* of his death, we shall be also in the *likeness* of his resurrection. (Romans 6:3-5)

Baptism not only is in *similitude* of the death, burial, and resurrection of Christ, it also *symbolizes* that the old self is crucified with him, and that being dead with Christ a person can be freed from sin and live with Christ. (Romans 6:1-10) Man is to be "buried with him in baptism, wherein also ye are risen with him through the faith of the operation of God, who hath raised him from the dead." (Colossians 2:12)

Man's baptism is a *likeness* of the baptism of Jesus Christ in that Christ "showeth unto the children of man that, according to the flesh he humbleth himself before the Father, and witness unto the Father that he would be obedient unto him in keeping all His commandments...he (Christ) having set the example before them." (2 Nephi 31:6-9) *Likewise* when a person is baptized he witnesses to the Father that he is willing to humble himself and follow the example set by the Savior by keeping all His commandments. As the Lord submitted himself to being baptized by John, he *represented* his obedience to His Father and His submission to being crucified. Christ is "He that ascended up on high, as also he descended below all things." (D & C 88:6) The Lord also showed His obedience as he condescended to come down from heaven and take upon himself mortal flesh: "he hath descended below them all." (D & C 122:8) *Likewise* man and women show their submission and acceptance of God's commandments as they covenant to obey the commandments upon being baptized.

The submission, condescencion and baptism of Christ was *symbolically* forecast as Jonah was swallowed and then vomited by the whale. "The waters compassed me about...I went down to the bottoms of the mountains...yet, thou brought up my life from corruption, O Lord my God. (Jonah 2:5-6) It is such an important symbol that the Lord said that there would be no *sign* given to the adulterous generation who seek signs "but the *sign* of the Prophet Jonas: For as Jonas was three days in the whale's belly; so shall the Son of Man be three days and three nights in the heart of the earth." (Matthew 12:40-41) Of this symbol Nephi said that the God of Abraham, Isaac, and Jacob yielded himself into the hands of wicked men, to be lifted up and crucified and buried in a sepulchure which the Prophet Zenos referred to when he "spake concerning the three days of darkness which should be a *sign* given of his death." (1 Nephi 19:10) Jonah was immersed in water in *similitude* to baptism and was cleansed *symbolically* as he was immersed in the water of the whale's belly and then brought up from a "life of corruption." The *sign* of Jonah *symbolized* the death, burial and resurrection of Jesus Christ as it is also a *symbol* of the baptism of men and women.

As a result of Jonah's refusal to "cry against" the City of Nineveh, the Lord caused the huge fish to swallow and vomit him. The *sign* of Jonah was a warning to the City of Nineveh so that they would repent of their sins. *Likewise* the *sign* of Jonah is a warning to all mankind that they should repent and be baptized, "For as Jonas was a *sign* unto the Ninevites, so shall also the Son of Man to this generation." (Luke 11:30)

Baptism is also a *symbol* of man's birth as he leaves his pre-mortal existence and enters mortality. There are several scriptures which refer to baptism as being "born again." Christ said that "Except a man be born of the water and of the Spirit he cannot enter in the kingdom of heaven." (John 3:5) As one enters the water and is buried under the water of baptism and emerges from the water, he *symbolizes* the rebirth of the pre-mortal spirit as it enters the unborn baby's body, is immersed in the water inside the mortal mother's womb, and then emerges as a newborn mortal child. Both baptism and the birth of a baby are in *similitude* of the "spiritual death" that came when Adam was cast out of the Garden of Eden. Spiritual death is a separation from the presence of the Father and Son. It occurs as the spirit leaves the premortal sphere and enters mortality when a child is born. (Alma 42:9; D & C 29:41)

As a symbol of the birth of a baby, baptism *represents* death, water, blood, spirit, and cleansing. The Book of Moses states:

> That by reason of transgression cometh the fall, which fall bringeth death, and inasmuch as ye were born into the world by water, and blood, and the spirit...*even so* ye must be born again into the kingdom of heaven, of water, and the Spirit, and be cleansed by blood, even the blood of mine Only Begotten; that ye might be sanctified from all sin....
>
> For by the water ye keep the commandment; by the Spirit ye are justified, and by the blood ye are sanctified. (Moses 6:58-60; 1 John 5:3-9)

Baptism is in *similitude* of the blood of the mother which is present when the mother carries and gives birth to a child. Both are in *remembrance* of the blood that Christ shed for mankind in order that the person baptized may witness unto the Father that he will always remember the Savior. (3 Nephi 18:11) A partial description of those who will receive exaltation states that:

They are they who received the testimony of Jesus, and believed his name and were baptized after the *manner of* his burial, being buried in the water in his name....

That by keeping the commandments they might be washed and cleansed from all their sins. (D & C 76:51-52; See also *Discourses of Young,* p. 159)

Water, of itself, will not wash away sin; neither will keeping the Lord's commandments, entirely. Baptism *symbolizes* the atoning blood of Jesus which cleanses from sin all of those who keep the Lord's commandments. They are thereby sanctified by his atoning sacrifice, so that they "may become holy, without spot" in *similitude* of Christ being without spot or blemish. (Moroni 10:32-33) Jesus said:

No unclean thing can enter into his (the Father's) kingdom; therefore, nothing entereth into his rest save it be those who have washed their garments in my blood, because of their faith, and the repentance of all their sins, and their faithfulness unto me unto the end. (3 Nephi 27:19-20; 1 John 1:7)

Baptism thus *represents* a person as he is "born again" as being literally transplanted or resurrected from a life of sin to a life of righteousness, of being born again into God's presence. "They are in spiritual death...and are buried in the water and come forth in the resurrection of the Spirit back into spiritual life" (*Doctrines of Salv.,* Vol. 2, pp. 223, 326) There is also a *parallel* between birth into this world and birth into the Kingdom of God. (*Doctrines of Salv.,* Vol. 2, p. 325) Birth is the gate by which the spirit enters mortal life. Baptism is the gate through which man must enter the kingdom of God. (2 Nephi 31:17; John 3:5)

Baptism into the Family of Christ

When a baby is born into mortality, he is born into a mortal family which, is in *similitude* of being born again by baptism into the family of The Church of Jesus Christ, with "the Savior as the Bridegroom and the church as the bride. Through baptism, then, we become children in that royal family with Jesus Christ as our Father." (Theodore M. Burton, *BYU Devotional* Oct. 26, 1983; D & C 109:72-74) As the baptized members are born again, they are *symbolically* and actually adopted into the family of Christ. (*Mormon Doctrine:* "Adoption," p.22) Mosiah said to the faithful saints: "And now because of the covenant which ye have made ye shall be called the children of Christ...therefore, ye are born to him and have become his sons and his daughters." (Mosiah 5:7)

In connection with the adoption an intimate name, Abba, for the Eternal Father was sometimes used: (*LDS Bible Dictionary,* p. 600) "Ye have received the spirit of adoption, whereby we cry Abba, Father...that we are the children of God: And if children, then heirs; heirs of God, and joint heirs with Christ." (Romans 8:14-17; Galatians 4:4-7) Thus the adoption through baptism into Christ's Church on earth is in *similitude* to the adoption into the Father's kingdom in heaven.

Baptism, an earthly ordinance, is also in *similitude* of the Godhead in heaven:

> This is he that came by water and blood, even Jesus Christ....For there are three that bear record in heaven, the Father, the Word, and the Holy Ghost: and these three are one. And there are three that bear witness in earth, the Spirit, and the water, and the blood; and these three agree in one. (1 John 5:4-8)

Of this scripture Theodore M. Burton, of the First Quorum of Seventy, said:

> Note again the symbolism. *Just as* the three persons in the Godhead constitute a unity of purpose, *so* the three elements of baptism constitute a unity which can bring us back into the presence of those Three in heaven. The unity of this baptism ordinance on earth *mirrors* in *symbolism* the unity in heaven." (*BYU Devotional* Oct. 26, 1983)

Baptism by Fire and the Holy Ghost

The Lord said: "Ye must be born again into the Kingdom of Heaven, of water, and of the spirit." (Moses 6:59) The baptism of the Spirit or Holy Ghost is performed separately from that of the water and is often *symbolized* as the baptism of fire and of the Holy Ghost. (Matthew 3:11; 2 Nephi 31:13, etc.) Fire is used to clean and purify metal during the refining process; *likewise* the iniquity and evil within a man or woman are burned and cleaned out by the Holy Ghost during the refining of his or her soul *as if* by fire. (Mosiah 27:24-28) Those to whom the Spirit of God comes down from heaven and encircles are thereby born of the Spirit. The Holy Ghost will fall on them and they will be filled *as with* fire as were Nephi and Lehi "encircled about, yea they were as if in the midst of a flaming fire." (Helaman 5:43-45) Such refining and purifying comes to a person after he or she has received the baptism of the Holy Ghost and during a lifetime of obedience to God's commandments.

The baptism or bestowal of the Holy Ghost is performed by the laying on of hands by an elder holding the Melchezidek Priesthood. The Lord said to Edward Partridge, an early church bishop and missionary, "You are called to preach my gospel...and I will lay my hand upon you by the hand of my servant Sidney Rigdon, and you shall receive my spirit, the Holy Ghost." (D & C 36:1-2) Thus the ordinance of laying on of hands is *symbolic* of the hands of the Lord by which He bestows the gifts and blessings on his children in various ordinances while the officiator *represents* the Lord.

The Lord came to John to be baptized: "And Jesus, when he was baptized, went up straightway out of the water; and lo, the heavens were opened unto him and he saw the Spirit of God descending *like* a dove and lighting upon him." (Matthew 3:16) "And the Holy Ghost descended in a bodily shape *like* a dove upon him." (Luke 3:22) Joseph Smith added:

> The *sign* of the dove was insituted before the creation of the world for a *witness* for the Holy Ghost, and the devil cannot come in the *sign* of a dove. The Holy Ghost is a personage and is in the form of a personage. It does not confine itself to the form of the dove but in the *sign* of the dove. The Holy Ghost cannot be transformed into a dove; but the *sign* of a dove was given to John to *signify* the truth of the deed, as the dove is an *emblem* or *token* of truth and innocence. (*History of Church*, Vol. 5, p. 261; *Jesus The Christ*, p. 150)

The *symbol* of a dove has become universal. Among some early records there is an illustration showing a crescent moon *representing* an ark resting on waters with a dove hovering over the ark and a rainbow circled over both. (*Pagan Christian*, p. 83) A dove was sent by Noah from the window of the ark, "to see if the waters were abated from off the face of the ground." (Genesis 8:6-13) The illustration appears to suggest that the dove may have been a *symbol* of the Holy Ghost hovering over the ark and guiding it safely during its journey.

The Lord commanded that when the women of Israel bore children they were required to offer a dove as an *emblem* of purity in order that certain sins would be cleansed from them. This was done in connection with the sacrifice of "the days of her purifying." There is considerable symbolism in the sacrifice inasmuch as the priest is making an atonement for her and the *representation* points to Christ and his atoning sacrifice.

> And when the days of her purifying are fulfilled for a son, or for a daughter, she shall bring a lamb of the first year for a burnt offering, and a young pigeon, or a turtle-dove, for a sin offering, unto the door of the tabernacle of the congregation, unto the priest....
>
> And if she be not able to bring a lamb, then she shall bring two turtles (turtle doves), or two young pigeons; the one for the burnt offering, and the other for a sin offering; and the priest shall make an atonement for her, and she shall be clean. (Leviticus 12:6-8)

Baptism of the Earth

Baptism is also a *symbol* in the creation, lifespan and death of the earth. Its birth is similar to all other births, the earth first being buried in water at the beginning of its creation. It came forth from the water as the dry land appeared and was later covered with all the beauties of the plant and animal kingdoms. It became polluted by the fall of Adam and the sins of mankind and was thus brought under the sentence of death. The fall caused by Adam was redeemed by the atonement of Christ, but the earth also needs redeeming as a result of the sins committed by the descendents of Adam. According to Orson Pratt:

> The Lord ordained the baptism or immersion of the earth in water as a justifying ordinance...that the sins which have corrupted it may be washed away from its face...and the rains came and overwhelmed the earth, and the dry land disappeared in the womb of the mighty water even as in the beginning. The waters were assuaged; the earth came forth clothed with innocence; *like* the

newborn child, having been baptized or born again from the ocean
flood; and thus the old earth was buried with all its deeds and
arose to newness of life, its sins being washed away, *even as* a
man has to be immersed in water to wash away his own personal
sins. (*Discourses of Pratt*, p. 369)

The earth's baptism and cleansing by water came by the flood in
the time of Noah. The earth became corrupted again, requiring a second
cleansing, and next time it is to be a baptism by the element of fire,
which will come to pass at the beginning of the millennium. A more
detailed description will be given in the chapter about the millennium.
Elder Orson Pratt said:

This is a *representation* of the baptism that is received by man
after he has been baptized in water; for he is then to be baptized
with fire and the Holy Ghost and all his sins entirely done away;
so the earth will be baptized with fire, and wickedness swept away
from its face so that the glory of God shall cover it. (*Discourses
of Pratt*, p. 370; see also 2 Peter 3:4-7)

Anyone who understands the symbols and representations of baptism,
as herein cited, will know that there can be no other method of baptism
than by immersion. Sprinkling, pouring or any other method is not
a baptism. They will also know that the correct baptism is an absolute
requirement for entrance through the gate into The Church of Jesus
Christ on earth as well as that of the celestial kingdom of heaven. Since
The Church of Jesus Christ of Latter-day Saints is the only church
that baptizes by the correct immersion and by the proper priesthood
authority, it has the only valid baptism on earth.

Chapter Nine

THE LORD'S COMMANDMENTS

The Sacrament as a Renewal of the Baptismal Covenants

Because no one but Jesus is perfect, everyone sins to a greater or lesser degree after he is baptized. It is not required to be rebaptized after each mistake, but the Lord has instituted the ordinance of the sacrament in order to permit men and women to *symbolically represent* their covenant of baptism, thus enabling them to renew the covenants they made in the waters of baptism. (*Mormon Doctrine*, "Sacrament," p. 594) The sacrament was instituted by the Lord "to serve essentially the same purposes served by the sacrifices of" Old Testament times (*Promised Messiah*, p. 431) The sacrifices *symbolically* pointed towards the coming crucifixion of the savior and the covenants required of those who would receive all the benefits of the Lord's atonement. *Likewise* the sacrament points toward the Lord's previous atonement and to the covenants made at baptism. The sacrament thus has a dual purpose as a renewal of our covenants and as we partake of it in remembrance of Christ and his atoning sacrifice:

> And as they were eating, Jesus took bread and brake it, and blessed it, and said, "Take, eat; this is in remembrance of my body which I give for a ransom for you.
>
> And he took the *cup*, and gave thanks and gave it to them, saying, Drink ye all of it. For this is in *remembrance* of my blood of the new testament. (JST Matthew 26:22-24, original text)

And Paul said, "For as often as you eat this bread and drink this cup, ye do *shew* the Lord's death till he come." (1 Corinthians 11:23-26)

Claims by some churches that the bread and wine are the actual body and blood of Christ are entirely false. They are "the *emblems* of the flesh and blood of Christ." (D & C 20:40) We eat of the bread in *remembrance* of the body of the Son as a testimony that we may always remember him. We drink of the wine (or water) in *remembrance* of the blood of the Son which was shed for man. (3 Nephi 18:10-11; D & C 20:79) Brigham Young said that the Latter-day Saints partake of the sacrament

> To *witness* unto the Father, to Jesus Christ, and to the angels that they are believers in and desire to follow him in the regeneration, keep his commandments, build up his kingdom, revere his name and serve him with an undivided heart, that they may be worthy to eat and drink with him in his Father's Kingdom. (*Discourses of Young*, p. 172)

The word "wine" is used in the sacramental prayer as the *emblem* for blood. The word used at the Last Supper was the "cup," not mentioning the contents. (Matthew 26:27) The cup is a *symbol* of Christ's agony in the Garden of Gethsemane, (*Signs and Symbols*, p. 298) based on Christ's words "O my Father, if this *cup* may not pass away from me, except I drink it, thy will be done." (Matthew 26:42) *Likewise* each person should partake of the sacrament with the same dedication to the will of the Father. Neither the wine nor the contents of the cup were what is today called fermented wine; rather, they would have been unfermented grape juice. Some Bible scholars have determined that the "new wine" spoken of by Luke is an unfermented wine or "Must," a rich refreshing beverage that can be kept for years but is non-intoxicating. A modern revelation indicates that other liquids can be appropriately substituted for wine in the sacramental service. (D & C 27:1-4) The key to the symbolism is in what the wine or water *represents* and not in the product used.

Partaking of the sacrament is also done in *remembrance* of Jesus Christ as the Bread of Life in *like manner* as manna was sent down from heaven as a *symbol* of Jesus Christ, being sent down to earth as

> ...the true bread from heaven.
> For the bread of God is he which cometh down from heaven, and giveth life unto the world...

if any man eat of this bread, he shall live forever, and the bread that I will give is my flesh, which I will give for the life of the world....

Whoso eateth my flesh, and drinketh my blood hath eternal life. (John 6:32,33,51,54)

By partaking of the manna, the Israelites were *symbolically* taught "that man doth not live by bread only, but by every word that proceedeth out of the mouth of the Lord doth man live." (Deuteronomy 8:3) Also *symbolically,* Paul taught that those who were baptized unto Moses "did all eat the same spiritual meat; And did all drink the same spiritual drink; for they drank of that spiritual Rock that followed them: and that Rock was Christ." (1 Cor. 10:2-4)

By being baptized and by partaking of the sacrament, a person *represents* that he believes in the Lord and Savior, and accepts His plan of salvation and will do those things necessary in order that he may be saved through the atonement of Christ. This principle was taught when the Lord told the Israelites that the destroying angel would pass them by if "they shall take of the blood and strike it on the two side posts and on the upper door post of the houses....And the blood shall be to you for a *token* upon the houses where ye are: and when I see the blood I will pass over you." (Exodus 12:7-13) Placing the blood on the doors was a *symbol* to those who accepted and obeyed, whereby they would be saved. Elder McConkie explained this event as

> *Signifying* that the blood of Christ, which should fall as drops in Gethsemane and flow in a stream from a pierced side as he hung on the cross, would cleanse and save the faithful. And that *as* those in Israel were saved temporarily because the blood of a sacrificial lamb was sprinkled on the doorposts of their houses, *so* the faithful of all ages would wash their garments in the blood of the Eternal Lamb and from him receive an eternal salvation. (*Promised Messiah*, pp. 429-431)

From this time forward the Israelites, or the Jews, have celebrated the Feast of the Passover each year to commemorate this event. Because circumcision was a *symbol* of the covenants the Israelites made, uncircumcised men who were not members of the Israelite "church" were not permitted to partake of the passover feast (Exodus 12:43) *Likewise* non-members of Christ's church in these latter days are not supposed to partake of the sacrament. In connection with the event, the Israelites were told not to eat leavened bread for seven days, "for whosoever eateth leavened bread from the first day until the seventh day, that soul shall be cut off from Israel." (Exodus 12:15) *Similarly,* to the extent that we do not keep the commandments of God we shall be cut off from the celestial kingdom.

Anointing and Administrations

The healing power of God is another principle of the gospel for which the saints are grateful, as it miraculously comes to them through the anointing and administrations to the sick by the laying on of hands of the priesthood. It is not to be supposed that there is a *counterpart* of the ordinance of administration in the kingdom of heaven, for sickness and disease are for this world only. But every one who becomes exalted in the celestial kingdom will be required to know all the aspects of sickness and disease and how to cure them, for that knowledge will be necessary in order to govern a world with millions of people on it.

Anointing with oil is common in the scriptiures as a *symbol* of being endowed with the Spirit or power of God. Moses used oil on Aaron's head "and anointed and sanctified him." (Leviticus 8:12) Peter said that "God anointed Jesus of Nazareth with the Holy Ghost and with power." (Acts 10:38) The apostles of the New Testament "anointed with oil many that were sick and healed them." (Mark 6:13) Some have questioned the use of olive oil for anointing in an administration, wondering why some other oil could not be used. The oil used must be a pure oil in order to *represent* the healing power of God. It was used in the lamps of the wise virgins as a *symbol* of their taking "the Holy Spirit for their guide." (D & C 45:57) Apparently the Lord chose the olive as being the purest, at least for the ordinances and symbols of the gospel. The olive leaf was brought back to the ark by the dove; the olive and olive tree are mentioned quite prominently in the Bible, and as a result have become an *emblem* of peace and purity throughout the world. (*Doctrines of Salv.*, Vol. 3, p. 180) Section 88 of the *Doctrine and Covenants* was *designated* as the Olive Leaf Revelation.

The Symbolism of God's Commandments

There are many doctrines of the Gospel and commandments of God that do not have specific symbolic counterparts in the next life except that they point to Christ and those things man must do in order for him to perfect himself and become as God. Some of the commandments are of a negative, or "Thou shalt not" nature, and *represent* those things the Eternal Father and Mother would not do. Each has a necessary purpose because they prepare a person for Godhead.

"Thou shalt have no other gods before me." There can be only one order of authority in the universe. Only those who accept that order wholeheartedly can have a place as a son of God in the universe. "Thou shalt not make unto thee any graven image." Money, idols, or other things of a material nature more often than not *represent* "graven images" and are worshipped more than God. "Thou shalt not take the name of the Lord thy God in vain." Certainly, as they prepare their millions of spirit offspring for earth life, neither the Eternal Father nor Mother use foul language.

"Remember the sabbath day, to keep it holy." The observance of the sabbath is a *witness* unto God of man's willingness to obey God's commandments. Spirit children as they are reared and instructed in their pre-mortal life will not be entrusted to the care of anyone who has not learned while in their mortal state the importance of sabbath observance and the spiritual needs of the spirit children. To help them learn the Lord said: "Thou shall go to the house of prayer and offer up thy sacraments upon my holy day; For verily this is a day appointed unto you to rest from your labors, and to pay thy devotions unto the Most High." (D & C 59:9-10) The sabbath day has been used as a symbol since the beginning of time. The earth was organized in six periods of time with the seventh period given to rest. The six days of labor with the sabbath day of rest *commemorated* this event from this time of Adam to Moses. (Exodus 20:8-11) From Moses's day to Christ's advent on earth it was a *reminder* that the Lord, "through a mighty hand and by a stretched out arm," brought the children of Israel out of Egyptian bondage. (Deuteronomy 5:12-15) Since the resurrection of Jesus Christ, the sabbath has been observed on the first day of the week commemorating that the resurrected Lord first appeared to others on Sunday, after coming forth from the grave. (John 20:1; Mark 16:9) From that time forth the saints of God have brought the Lord's sacrifice to mind on the Lord's day as a *reminder* that only through observance of his day and keeping his covenants they may become like him and someday dwell with him.

"Honor thy father and thy mother" *represents* the love and honor those who gain exaltation as sons and daughters of the Eternal Father and Mother will have for Them in the celestial kingdom. It also *symbolizes* the love and honor those who gain celestial glory will still hold for the parents they had during earth life who also gain eternal life.

"Thou shalt not kill." Anyone who cannot control his emotions enough to avoid bloodshed cannot expect to enter a kingdom of glory where the righteous dwell, let alone have governing powers over others. The Eternal Father and Mother possess perfect attitudes of love and harmony.

"Thou shalt not commit adultery." Anyone entrusted in the hereafter with billions of spirits cannot have evil sexual desires. There can be no place for the breaking up of families in the Celestial Kingdom. The Lord's law of chastity is next in importance to that of the commandment "Thou shalt not kill."

"Thou shalt not steal." Who would enjoy a celestial kingdom where anyone was allowed to steal from his neighbor? There will be no need for policing, for anyone who gains entrance into celestial glory will have overcome any desire to covet that which is not his own. The same applies to the commandment "Thou shalt not bear false witness," for there can be no lying in heaven.

"Thou shalt not be idle; for he that is idle shall not eat the bread nor wear the garments of the laborer." (D & C 42:42) It takes little imagination to realize that those who spend a life of inactivity and indifference will be incapable of being a God. They cannot be slothful servants; they must learn to "do many things of their own free will....For the power is in them, wherein they are agents unto themselves." (D & C 58:27-29)

Adversity and Service Develops Talents

Man must learn to meet and overcome every obstacle in order to be capable of ruling a heavenly kingdom. Certainly the Father encountered many obstacles in forming a universe. The strength developed from adversity in this life is a *counterpart* of the strength needed as an exalted being. Dr. Norman Vincent Peale said:

> It could be that the world was made as it is, full of problems and difficulty, to bring out a tough quality in human beings. What

is almighty God attempting to do with us? There must be some purpose, else it's a huge, grim joke and not so funny at that. I wonder if his purpose isn't to make strong, controlled people, who can handle life on earth so well that they derive eternal life.... (*Deseret News*, April 30, 1962)

It will take very high motivation for a person to develop his talents enough to gain exaltation; he will be expected to develop as many as possible while here on earth. The Lord pointed this out when he gave the Parable of the Talents. In it He said, "the kingdom of heaven is *as a* man traveling into a far country." The man called his servants and gave to one of them five talents, to another two, and to another one, each according to his own ability. When he returned, the first two had gained other talents while the one who had been given only one talent had wasted his time and had not even developed that talent. The lord of the servants commended the two who had gained upon their talents and told them they would be rulers over many things, but of the other he said: "Take therefore the talent from him, and give it unto him which hath ten talents." (Matthew 25:15-28) Although this parable encompasses all types of talents, it is more specifically *symbolic* of the talents developed through service in church callings. The recipients of the talents in the parable

...were his own servants whom the Master had called. They were His goods with which He entrusted them before leaving for a "far country."

The Lord has left to be with His Father. He has left His kingdom in the hands of His servants. To some He has entrusted five talents, some two, some one. Some are called as General Authorities, some as bishops, some as stake missionaries, some as home or visiting teachers. ("Viewpoint," *Church News*, June 20, 1987)

Everyone enters mortality with talents that were founded in premortal life, but these talents must be nurtured and developed or they will die. All talents developed in mortality will have their *counterpart* in heaven because everyone will take their personal talents with them. There are people who are born with many talents that will lose them through disuse, while others born with few noticeable talents surpass the more gifted through hard work and initiative. In other words, all those who do their best with the talents they have will not only develop and perfect those talents but will receive and develop others, while those who do not use what they have will lose them.

The parable of the five wise versus the five foolish virgins aptly *symbolizes* the urgency of continual service in the church and the development of our talents in order to be ready when Christ comes. "Then shall the kingdom of heaven by *likened* unto ten virgins which took their lamps and went forth to meet the bridegroom." The five that "were foolish, took their lamps and took no oil with them: But the wise took oil in their vessels with their lamps." While waiting for him "they all slumbered and slept." Then at midnight the Bridegroom came. The lamps of the foolish virgins had gone out, while the five "that were ready went in with him to the marriage: and the door was shut." (Matthew 25:1-13)

The symbolism is plain. The bridegroom *is* (*represents*) the Lord, whose second coming has so long been awaited (as waited the virgins). The wedding *is* (*represents*) His kingdom. The bridesmaids (virgins) are His disciples. The lamps are a *symbol* of their discipleship (church membership), the oil the individual, personal preparation essential to make the lamps burn. ("Viewpoint," *Church News*, June 20, 1987)

At the last minute the foolish virgins wanted the others to share their oil with them, but such was impossible. *Likewise* each of us is responsible for his own oil. We may through certain church service lead, guide, and direct others, but it is up to each person to develop his or her own talents and capabilities. *Symbolically* as with the ten virgins when the hour of Christ's coming arrives, it will be too late to go back and serve in the Lord's church.

The Importance of a Healthy Mind and Body

Because it is eternal, The Church of Jesus Christ places a great emphasis on education. The Lord said: "Whatsoever principle of intelligence we attain unto in this life, it will rise with us in the resurrection. And if a person gains more knowledge and intelligence in this life through his diligence and obedience than another, he will have so much the advantage in the world to come." (D & C 130:18-19)

Thus if one studies astronomy, chemistry, geology, mathematics, languages, art, cooking or any other field of knowledge and truth it will add to his understanding of the great system of universal truth that exists in the universe. In fact, today's knowledge is a mere symbol compared to that which will be revealed in our lifetime. (See *Discourses of Pratt*, p. 41) *Likewise*, the knowledge an individual attains in his lifetime is a mere symbol to that which he can gain in his post-mortal life. Speaking to members of the church, Brigham Young said: "I expect if I am faithful, with yourselves, that I shall see the time that we shall know how to prepare to organize an earth like this; how to people the earth; how to redeem it, how to sanctify it, and how to glorify it." (*Discourses of Young*, p. 97)

Another important principle to the salvation of mankind is a commandment given by revelation known as the "Word of Wisdom," parts of which follow: "That inasmuch as any man drinketh wine or strong drink among you, behold it is not good...And again, tobacco is not for the body, neither for the belly...And again, hot drinks are not for the body or belly." (D & C 89:5-8) The hot drinks here mentioned were later specified by the Prophet Joseph and others as tea and coffee. "I understand that some of the people are excusing themselves in using tea and coffee because the Lord only said 'hot drinks.' Tea and coffee are what the Lord meant when he said 'hot drinks.'" (*Word of Wisdom*, pp. 85-86)

Many people argue that such a small thing as drinking a cup of tea or coffee will not keep them out of the celestial kingdom, but one of the requirements for entering the temple is that the participant obey the Word of Wisdom. The temple is the Lord's House here on earth. It is a *symbolical counterpart* of the Father's kingdom in heaven; so if a person cannot enter the temple because of an unwillingness to observe the Word of Wisdom, he cannot expect to gain admittance into the celestial glory where God and Christ dwell. The Lord said that no unclean thing can inherit the kingdom of God or dwell in His presence. (Moses 6:57) The Word of Wisdom thus becomes a *symbol* of the purity one must attain in order to dwell with our Eternal Father in a celestial kingdom.

Tithing and Service to Others

Tithing, a tenth of one's income, was practiced in Old Testament times. (Leviticus 27:30-32) Again, in these latter days the Lord has revealed the doctrine of tithing: "And after that, those who have thus been tithed shall pay one-tenth of all their interest annually." (D & C 119:4) All worthy members of the church are expected to pay one-

tenth of their income to the church. Just as tithing is a requirement
to acquire a recommend to enter the temple, it is necessary for entrance
into the highest degree of the celestial kingdom. It is so important that
the Lord has said that those who rob God by not paying a tithe will
be "cursed with a curse," but for those who bring their tithes to the
storehouse the Lord will "Open you the windows of heaven, and pour
out a blessing, that there shall not be room to receive it." (Malachi
3:8-10) And they "shall not be burned at his coming." (D & C 64:23)
Tithing is a reliable test of faith. A person proves to the Lord that he
is not weak in the faith but is willing to share what he has with the
Lord. It is a firm anchor to the church. It teaches a person economy
and thrift.

Tithing, however, is a lesser order and a preparation for a principle
of the gospel known as the "United Order" or law of consecration.
(D & C 104) The purpose of the United Order was to establish an
equality of earthly or physical blessings wherein everyone would have
all his particular temporal needs fulfilled. Under the United Order,
all goods and property were to be turned in to the Church and then,
according to the capability and needs of the family or individual, the
individuals were placed as stewards over specific properties or jobs
or businesses. Then, as needed, food, clothing or other goods could
be drawn from the central warehouse. The law of consecration (United
Order) is the earthly *counterpart* of a basic system in the priesthood
organization of the universe which the inheriters of celestial glory must
of necessity learn in order to be able to govern as sons and daughters
of the Eternal Father. They will be given a stewardship over whatever
"mansions," worlds or stellar systems they need in order to function
at the progress level they have attained in the celestial kingdom.

A basic purpose of the law of consecration is to teach material equality
among the inhabitants of the earth in *similitude* of the equality that
will exist in heaven, "That you may be equal in the bonds of heavenly
things, yea, and earthly things also, for the obtaining of heavenly things.
For if ye are not equal in earthly things ye cannot be equal in obtaining
heavenly things." (D & C 78:3-8) Tithings, fast offerings and
participating in the Church Welfare System teaches to a lesser degree
some of the principles of equality found in the law of consecration.

Another basic principle of the gospel is service to others. It is doubtful
that anyone can perform any activity in the church without directly

or indirectly serving someone else. Those who unselfishly give of their time in service do so in *similitude* of the service Christ gave to all mankind. "Verily I say unto you, inasmuch as ye have done it unto the least of these my brethren, ye have done it unto me." (Matthew 25:40) Service is in *similitude* to a person laying down his life for others *as* did Christ on the cross. "And whoso layeth down his life in my cause, for my name sake, shall find it again even life eternal." (D & C 98:13) After Christ had washed the disciples' feet, he told them that it was an *example* that they should do to one another as he had done to them. (John 13:5, 14-16)

Many of those who serve, such as teachers, missionaries, and leaders are *represented* in the scriptures as shepherds, while those whom they serve are *symbolized* as sheep. As shepherds they labor with the sheep who are members of Christ's church, especially the wayward ones, in *similitude to* the Lord's labors as a shepherd over His sheep or flock:

> As a shepherd seeketh out his flock that are scattered; so will I seek out my sheep...And I will set up one shepherd over them, and he shall feed them...and he shall be their shepherd. (Ezekiel 34:12, 23; Isaiah 40:11; John 10:2)

And also,

> For the Son of Man is come to save that which is lost. How think ye? If a man have an hundred sheep and one of them be gone astray, doth he not leave the ninety and nine and goeth into the mountain, and seek that which is gone astray? (Matthew 18:10-14)

The shepherd's staff adds meaning to the service one renders as a shepherd in that the staff of a shepherd is "a *symbol* of office and authority," (Webster's Dictionary) and the crook in his staff *represents* "a loving arm, and an understanding heart." (Ezra T. Benson, *Church News*, April 11, 1987)

The Lord has given prayer for a bonding link between Him and man to help us keep God's commandments. The "Lord's Prayer" says "Thy kingdom come. Thy will be done in earth *as* it is in heaven." (Matthew 6:10) Prayer is one of the most essential principles of the gospel that will be used in heaven. Without it man could not communicate with the Father, which is essential to reach any eternal goal. Certainly if there is no prayer in heaven, the prayers of mankind are in *similitude* of whatever type of communication there is between the Father and his sons and daughters in the kingdom of heaven.

Chapter Ten

THE FAMILY SEALED FOR
TIME AND ETERNITY

The Patriarchal Order of the Priesthood

In an earlier chapter, the patriarchal order of the priesthood among the Gods of the universe was discussed, whereby an Eternal Father would rule as patriarch over his sons and they in turn over their sons, including their individual dominions. The patriarchal order of the family on earth is the *counterpart* of the heavenly organization.

The church and religious activities were governed by patriarchal authority from the time of Adam until Moses. As the patriarch or prophet died, his oldest son was chosen to take his place. However, the patriarchal priesthood encompassed more than the leaders of the church; it was an intregal part of each individual family organization. The father was head of his household and ruler of his family. (*Perfection*, pp. 113-114) Although church activities are no longer governed by the patriarchal family, the family organization and responsibilities have not changed. As one holding the priesthood under the patriarchal order on earth, the father holds his place as head of his family; he is the patriarch over his sons and daughters and they over their children, each in his proper order, in *similitude* of the patriarchal order in heaven:

> Every family is a kingdom, a nation, a government, within itself, to a certain extent; and the head of the family is the legislator, the judge, the governor. This is what constitutes the Patriarchal office and was originally the sole government for all the inhabitants on this earth....

And for that matter, every man is a patriarch who is the natural father or head of a family, if his children have been born to him under the bond of the Holy Priesthood. (*Priesthood Government*, pp. 82, 269)

The family on earth is a family in heaven in miniature. Earth is the place where the family organizations are first begun. Those who are going to continue to have the joys of family life in the future which they have in this life, must labor to perpetuate them. The family here is *in similitude* of the family there, and the experiences of family life on earth are to teach people how to live in a patriarchal family organization in the celestial kingdom. One experiences in this life to a minor degree the love that Father and Mother in heaven have for their children. The love between the Eternal Father and Mother in heaven is a *counterpart*, but more refined and stronger than that which exists between a husband and wife on earth.

The Proper Marriage and Sealing

The Eternal Father has established very rigid and specific requirements for those who will inherit positions of glory in the patriarchal order of the universe. Of major importance is the proper marriage ceremony and the sealing of it by the Holy Spirit of Promise. The Lord declared:

> In the celestial glory there are three heavens or degrees:
> And in order to obtain the highest, a man must enter in this order of the priesthood; (meaning the new and everlasting covenant of marriage).
> And if he does not, he cannot obtain it.
> He may enter into the other, but that is the end of his kingdom; he cannot have an increase. (D & C 131:1-4)

He has also said:

> And again, verily I say unto you, if a man marry a wife by my word, which is my law, and by the new and everlasting covenant, and it is sealed unto them by the Holy Spirit of promise, by him who is anointed, unto whom I have appointed this power, and the keys of this priesthood; and it shall be said unto them...ye shall inherit thrones, kingdoms, principalities, and

powers, dominions, all heights and depths,...it shall be done unto them in all things whatsoever my servant hath put upon them, in time and through all eternity, and shall be of full force when they are out of the world, and they shall pass by the angels and the Gods, which are set there, to their exaltaion and glory in all things, as hath been sealed upon their heads, which glory shall be a fulness and continuation of the seeds forever and ever. (D & C 132:19)

The marriage covenant, spoken of by the Lord in the above scripture, is the sealing of a couple in a temple of the Lord for time and all eternity, by one who holds the keys of authority to perform eternal marriages. There is no other way for a couple to be husband and wife in post-mortal life. It is in *similitude* of the permanent marriage relationship between the Eternal Father and Mother in heaven. In contrast, the Lord said:

Therefore, if a man marry him a wife in the world, and he marry her not by me, nor by my word; and he covenant with her so long as he is in the world, and she with him, their covenant and marriage are not of force when they are dead, and when they are out of the world. (D & C 132:15)

Thus the marriages performed by civil authorities or by anyone outside of the temples of the Lord are *symbols* of an incomplete or unbinding contract in that they terminate at the death of one of the participants.

Therefore when they are out of this world they neither marry nor are given in marriage; but are appointed angels in heaven, which angels are ministering servants, to minister unto those who are worthy of a far more, and exceeding, and an eternal weight of glory.

For these angels did not abide by my law, therefore, they cannot be enlarged, but remain separately and singly without exaltation in their saved condition, to all eternity, and from henceforth are not Gods, but as angels of God, forever and ever. (D & C 132:16-17)

Paul wrote of those who would attain less than eternal exaltation, "Are they not all ministering spirits sent for to minister for them who shall be heirs of salvation." (Hebrews 1:14)

The Relationship Between Husband and Wife

Paul *symbolized* the marriage relationship of husband and wife, comparing it to the relationship between the Church and Christ:

> Wives, submit yourselves unto your own husbands, as unto the Lord.
>
> For the husband is the head of the wife, even as Christ is the head of the church; and he is savior of the body.
>
> Therefore as the church is subject unto Christ, so let the wives be to their own husbands in everything. Husbands, love your wives, *even as* Christ also loved the church, and gave himself to it. (Ephesians 5:22-25)

The husband is head of the wife and family because he holds the priesthood as does Christ, but the husband, through his love, is to give himself to his wife, as did Christ to the church. The church *represents* the bride, the savior the bridegroom. (D & C 109:72-74; Matthew 9:15) However, the wife is not a servant to the husband neither is the husband expected to be dominated by the wife. The role of the wife in the relationship to her husband, and he to her, has been determined by the Father. According to the scriptures, each has his and her particular responsibilities:

In the Garden of Eden, Eve was declared as the help meet for Adam. The wife is to comfort and delight her husband, (D & C 25:5, 14) and revere him. (Ephesians 5:33) Her desires are to be to her husband, (Moses 4:22) and she is to be in subjection to him. (1 Peter 3:1) Mothers are to teach their children the way they should go. (Alma 56:47)

A husband shall love his wife with all his heart (Ephesians 5:25) and covet no others. (Mosiah 13:24) The husband is the head of the wife, (Ephesians 5:23) but he is to honor her "as unto the weaker vessel, and as being heirs together." (1 Peter 3:7) The wife has claim on her husband for maintenance, (D & C 83:2) and he is responsible for the sacred support to her and the children. (Alma 44:5) He is also to fight for them if necessary (Mormon 2:23) and to set a good example. (Jacob 2:35)

The above duties *represent* the respective activities of the Eternal Father and Mother in heaven, but marriage is a joint endeavor and neither a man nor a woman can be exalted without the other. "The same pure feelings of love that exist in the bosoms of the male and female in this world will exist with sevenfold intensity in the next world, governed by the law of God; there will be no corruptions or infringements, upon one another's rights." (*Discourses of Pratt*, p. 373)

But with marriage there are profound responsibilities. The husband and wife must not only live lives worthy of exaltation, but they also must teach their children to do the same, in *similitude* of the teaching that they as heavenly parents will do as they instruct their spirit offspring. There are many scriptures containing admonitions from the Lord that parents are to teach their children gospel principles. (Dueteronomy 4:9; Proverbs 22:6; Mosiah 4:15) If the parents wait for their children to grow to maturity before they choose for themselves what they will do, they will have little gospel foundation upon which to base a comparison with the worldly teachings of Satan. Teaching children correct gospel principles is so important that the Lord has said that if it is not done "the sin be upon the heads of their parents." (D & C 68:25, 28)

Ordinances Must Be Sealed for Validity

All ordinances performed on earth must be "Sealed by the Holy Spirit of Promise" before they are valid in heaven:

> And verily I say unto, that—All covenants, contracts, bonds, obligations, oaths, vows, performances, connections, associations, or expectations, that are not made, and entered into and sealed by the Holy Spirit of promise, of him who is anointed...are of no efficacy, virtue or force, in and after the resurrection from the dead. (D & C 132:7)

Also,

> Those who reach celestial glory are those who have kept all the commandments, "And who overcome by faith, and are sealed by the Holy Spirit of promise, which the Father sheds forth upon all those who are just and true." (D & C 76:53)

When an officiator performs an ordinance of the gospel he, insofar as the church kingdom of God on earth is concerned, seals that ordinance. The words *seal* and *sealings* are often used in administrations, baptisms, temple marriages, ordinations, endowments, and sealing of children to parents. However, these sealings are in *similitude* of the greater sealing that will be done by the Holy Ghost. All earthly ordinances are valid insofar as the church is concerned, but they are only valid in heaven if the person has lived worthy of them and the Holy Spirit has verified it by the sealing. People may on the surface look as if they are keeping the commandments of God, yet inside be evil or indifferent. The sealing by the Holy Ghost is based on a person's worthiness and thus becomes a safeguard whereby no one is able to receive that which he is not entitled to.

We may deceive men but we cannot deceive the Holy Ghost and our blessings will not be eternal unless they are also sealed by the Holy Spirit of promise, the Holy Ghost, one who reads the thoughts and hearts of men and give his sealing of approval to the blessings pronounced upon their heads. (Melvin J. Ballard, *Sermons*, p. 237)

Chapter Eleven

LIFE IN THE SPIRIT WORLD

Spirit Life is Much the Same as Earth Life

At the point at which someone dies, the spirit of the person leaves his mortal body. The body disintegrates, but the spirit goes to a state or place called the spirit world where spirits remain until the time to be resurrected. (Alma 40:21) Since the mind belongs to the spirit and not to the mortal remains, the spirit individual will continue to act and think in much the same manner as he did in mortality. (Alma 34:34) However, "A veil is drawn between the one sphere and the other whereby all the objects in the spiritual sphere are rendered invisible to those in the temporal." (*Key to Theology*, p. 125; For more detail see *Temples*, 1945 ed., pp. 303-305; 1968 ed., pp. 335-337)

Brigham Young said that those in the spirit world are mingling with each other there in clans and societies as people do here, and that their thoughts, desires and activities are much the same. (*Discourses of Brigham Young*, pp. 378-380) Lynn McKinley explains the purpose:

> In the intermediary spirit state there is still a continuation of the processes of trial and proving to take place to see how far men will accept and live the Gospel, or those points of the Gospel not presented to them or comprehended by them while on the earth...that they may by merit earn for themselves the glory they receive in the final judgment.... (*Life Eternal*, p. 113)

The Prophet Joseph Smith said: "It is not all to be comprehended in this world; it will be a great work to learn our salvation and exaltation even beyond the grave." *The Vision* p. 20)

There are two different states or conditions into which people will be placed in the spirit world; paradise for the righteous and hell for those who have been wicked. Alma said that

> ...the spirits of all men whether they be good or evil, are taken home to that God who gave them life. And then shall it come to pass, that the spirits of those who are righteous are received unto a state of happiness, which is called paradise, a state of rest, a state of peace...
>
> that the spirits of those who are wicked shall be cast into outer darkness...
>
> thus they remain in this state, as well as the righteous in paradise, until the time of resurrection. (Alma 40:11-14)

The State of the Wicked

The state of the wicked is *symbolized* by the word "hell". The Lord revealed that "These are they who are cast down to hell and suffer the wrath of Almighty God, until the fullness of times when Christ shall have subdued all enemies under his feet, and shall have perfected his work." (D & C 76:106; See 1 Nephi 15:34-35) Hell is that part of the spirit world inhabited by the wicked while awaiting the day of their resurrection. There they suffer the torments of the damned; there they welter in the vengeance of eternal fire. According to Alma, they are they who have been "taken captive by the devil, and led by his will down to destruction. Now this is what is *meant* by the chains of hell." (Alma 12:11) The fire and brimstone spoken of in the scriptures does not mean fire in the general term of physical science, but they are *symbolic* descriptions of the state of mind that a person is in while he or she undergoes the tortures of hell. Joseph Smith said: "A man is his own tormenter and his own condemner. Hence the saying, they shall go into the lake that burns with fire and brimstone. The torment of disappointment in the mind of man is *as* exquisite *as* a lake burning with fire and brimstone. I say, *so* is the torment of man." (*Teachings* p. 357)

Because of evil practices and the loss of the spirit of God, there are many in the world today that discover the torment of their minds to be so great they cannot bear to live and many commit suicide. The torment experienced in this life will be far less than that of its *counterpart* in hell. Such torment was experienced by the rich man as he lifted up his eyes from hell and said "I am tormented in this flame." (Luke 16:24)

The hell experienced in the spirit world is not only a punishment, but it may serve as a means of rehabilitation; it may be a process of cleansing. (*Perfection*, p. 304) and "the prisoner may come forth from the prison, when the uttermost farthing is paid." (*Doctrines of Salv.*, Vol. 2, p. 131; D & C 128:22) Elder Bruce McConkie said:

> The particular sense in which hell is spirit prison is in that those who there dwell are imprisoned by darkness, unbelief, ignorance, sin, and the chains of hell. As rapidly as they can overcome these obstacles—gain light, believe truth, acquire intelligence, cast off sin, and break the chains of hell—they can leave the hell that imprisons them and dwell with the righteous in the peace of paradise. (*Mormon Doctrine:* "Spirit Prison," p. 682)

But such will be difficult. There will be an increased activity of the spirit mind in the spirit world. Death will not change the attitude, goals, likes, or habits of the spirit as it passes through the veil except that "We will find when we are dead every desire, every feeling will be greatly intensified." (Elder Melvin J. Ballard, *Three Degrees*, p. 12; *Discourses of Young*, p. 379) This statement means both good, bad, and indifferent feelings will be intensified. Those that have been righteous will increase in their faithfulness, purity and intelligence, while to those that are wicked "The memories of their former sins will also be sharp and clear, but if they have rejected their means of being saved from their sins and have gloried in their wickedness, those memories of their former evil deeds will produce only a vastly increased hardness and rebellion and bitterness within them." (*Life Eternal*, p. 122)

Also the power and influence of Satan will be felt in the spirit world *as* it is in mortality. Brigham Young said:

> Those who have died without the gospel are continually afflicted by those evil spirits. (*Temples*, 1945 ed., p. 308) And when you are in the spirit world, everything will appear as natural as things now do...and you will learn that they (the evil spirits) are striving with all their might—laboring and toiling diligently as any

individual would, to accomplish an act in this world—to destroy the children of men. (*Discourses of Young*, p. 380)

The State of the Righteous

But concerning the faithful Saints of the Church of Jesus Christ, Brigham Young said:

> If we are faithful in our religion, when we go into the spirit world, the fallen spirits—Lucifer and the third part of the heavenly hosts that come with him, and the spirits of wicked men who have dwelt upon this earth, the whole of them combined will have no influence over our spirits. Is not this an advantage? Yes, all the rest of the children of men are more or less subject to them, and they are subject to them as they were while here in the flesh. (*Discourses of Young*, p. 379)

The Intermediate State of Spirits

The great majority of mankind will not be ready candidates entitled to enter the spirit world Paradise at their death, nor will they be consigned to the spirit world Hell. They are located in the spirit world in an area called the spirit prison. Located there are all those who need to be taught the gospel and to do all those things necessary to prepare them for the celestial glory or to whatever glory they will be able to attain.

It is of the latter group that Christ was speaking when He said to the thief on the cross, "Today shalt thou be with me in paradise" (*meaning* the world of spirits). (*Teachings*, p. 309) After His death and before His resurrection, Christ went and preached unto the spirits in an intermediate state *symbolized* as a prison. (D & C 76:73) Apostle Peter spoke of this occasion:

> For Christ...being put to death in the flesh, but quickened by the spirit: By which also he went and preached unto the spirits in prison;
> Which sometime were disobedient, when once the longsuffering of God waited in the days of Noah, while the ark was preparing, wherein few, that is, eight souls were saved by water. (1 Peter 3:18-20)

Peter also taught that

> For for this cause was the gospel preached also to them that are dead, that they might be judged according to men in the flesh, but live according to God in the spirit. (1 Peter 4:6)

After reading these scriptures, the late President Joseph F. Smith received the following vision:

> As I pondered over these things which are written, the eyes of my understanding were opened, and the Spirit of the Lord rested upon me, and I saw the hosts of the dead, both small and great....
>
> The son of God appeared declaring liberty to the captives who had been faithful, and there he preached to them the everlasting gospel, the doctrine of the resurrection and redemption of mankind from the fall, and from individual sins on conditions of repentance....
>
> I perceived that the Lord went not in person among the wicked and disobedient who had rejected the truth, to teach them;
>
> but behold, from among the righteous he organized his forces and appointed messengers, clothed with power and authority, and commissioned them to go forth and carry the light of the gospel to them that were in darkness, even to all the spirits of men....
>
> Thus was the gospel preached to those who had died in their sins without a knowledge of the truth or in transgression, having rejected the prophets.
>
> These were taught faith in God, repentance from sin, vicarious baptism or the remission of sins, the gift of the Holy Ghost by the laying on of hands, and all other principles of the gospel that were necessary for them to know in order to qualify themselves that they might be judged according to men in the flesh but live according to God in the spirit. (D & C 138:11, 18-19, 29-30, 32-34)

The same organization is used to carry out the Lord's work in the spirit world as here on earth; men will hold the same priesthood as they do here, and they will be the ones who will carry the gospel to the spirits in prison and labor with them. President Woodruff said:

> Every man who is faithful in his quorum here will join his quorum there. When a man dies and his body is laid in the tomb, he does not lose his position. The Prophet Joseph Smith held

the keys of this dispensation on this side of the veil, and he will hold them throughout the countless ages of eternity. (*Temples*, 1945 ed., p. 282; 1968 ed., p. 313; *Journal of Discourses*, Vol. 22, pp. 333-335)

Everyone to Hear the Gospel

Mortal life is the time and place to accept the gospel of Jesus Christ and to conform to all the ordinances and commandments prescribed by the Lord. But the great majority of mankind have never heard of the gospel. Of these people the Lord revealed to the Prophet Joseph Smith:

> All who have died without a knowledge of the gospel, who would have received it if they had been permitted to tarry, shall be heirs of the celestial kingdom of God; also, all that shall die hence forth without a knowledge of it, who would have received it with all their hearts, shall be heirs of that kingdom, for I, the Lord, will judge all men according to their works, according to the desire of their hearts. (*Teachings*, p. 107)

There are some who interpret the above paragraph to mean that all those who died without a knowledge of the gospel will need to do is to accept the gospel in the spirit world. But what will determine the desire of their hearts? It is determined on the same basis as here on earth. If the person is one who would have received the gospel with all his heart as he heard it while on earth, he will accept and keep all the commandments as they are presented to him in the spirit world. The Lord is thus able to judge him on the same basis and upon the same principles both in this life and in the spirit world. President Joseph F. Smith said:

> It stands to reason that, while the gospel may be preached unto all, the good and the bad, or rather to those who would repent and to those who would not repent in the spirit world, the *same as* it is here, redemption will only come to those who repent and obey. (*Sermons*, p. 246)

And also,

> You cannot take a murderer, a suicide, an adulterer, a liar, and simply by the performance of an ordinance of the Gospel, cleanse

him from sin and usher him into the presence of God. God has not instituted a plan of that kind, and it cannot be done....The wicked will have to repent of their wickedness. Those who died without the knowledge of the Gospel will have to come to the knowledge of it, and those who sin against light will have to pay the uttermost farthing for their transgression and their departure from the Gospel, before they ever get back to it. (*Temples*, 1945 ed., p. 333)

When those in the spirit world have accepted the gospel, have repented of their misdeeds and have paid the penalty for them, they are entitled to come out of the prison house. They must, however, not only accept the gospel, they also must accept all the ordinances of the gospel. "They, as well as the living, must comply with the law." (*Way to Perfection*, p. 39)

Many of the Lord's commandments can be obeyed while in the spirit world, but baptism, priesthood ordinations, temple endowments, and sealings, etc., are mortal ordinances and must be performed on the earth by those in authority in The Church of Jesus Christ of Latter-day Saints. They cannot be performed in the spirit world by spirits beings. (*Discourses of Young*, pp. 405-408) The priesthood of the universe has provided a way by which these ordinances may be performed. Someone here on earth acts as proxy and stands in the place of the one who has passed into the spirit world for whatever ordinance is to be performed. If the ordinance to be desired is baptism, the one performing the ordinance takes the individual who is acting as proxy into the water and baptizes him for, and in the name of, the one for whom the baptism is performed. This ordinance is called "baptism for the dead." A similar procedure is used for all other ordinances necessary for the deceased person. There is ample evidence among historians that baptism for the dead was practiced in early Christian churches, (1 Corinthians, 15:29; *History of Baptism for the Dead in Pristine Christianity*) but it, like many other ordinances and doctrines, was perverted or purged from the church. According to records of the Council of Carthage, in 397 A.D. there were many still practicing vicarious baptisms for the dead. (*U G & H*, April 1933, p. 63)

Some people claim that ordinances by proxy cannot be; they claim it is impossible for one person to be a proxy for another. This attitude is surprising, for vicarious proxy is common. Christ stood proxy for all mankind when he was crucified for their sins. Many proxies are voted in corporation matters. Individuals stand as proxies for a bride or a groom in civil marriage ceremonies when one or the other is in another country. Christ was sent to earth as an example so that as men follow in his footsteps they may become like him. Those who act as proxies in the saving labor of temple and genealogical activities do so in *similitude* to the vicarious labor of Jesus Christ. They

> Have a work to do just as important in its sphere as the Savior's work was in its sphere. Our fathers cannot be made perfect without us, we cannot be made perfect without them. They have done their work and now sleep. We are now called upon to do ours; which is the greatest work man ever performed on earth. Millions of our fellow creatures who have lived upon the earth and died without a knowledge of the Gospel, must be officiated for in order that they may inherit eternal life. (That is, all who would have received the gospel). (*Discourses of Young,* p. 406)

Those who labor in genealogical and temple services become "Saviors" in *similitude* to Christ's service as Savior to mankind. Of them Obediah said, "And Saviors shall come up on Mount Zion... and the kingdom shall be the Lord's." (Obediah 1:21) Mount Zion is *symbolic* of deliverance and holiness, (Obediah 1:17) and the Prophet Joseph Smith said such individuals are going to become Saviors on Mount Zion:

> By building their temples, erecting their baptismal fonts, and going forth and receiving all the ordinances, baptisms, confirmations, washings, anointings, ordinations and sealing powers upon their heads, in behalf of all their progenitors who are dead, and redeem them that they may come forth in the first resurrection and be exalted to thrones of glory with them; and herein is the chain that binds the hearts of the fathers to the children, and the children to the fathers, which fulfills the mission of Elijah. (*Teachings,* p. 330)

The mission of Elijah is that "...he shall turn the hearts of the fathers to the children, and hearts of the children to their fathers...." (Malachi 4:5-6) The "fathers to the children" *represent* ancestors who have passed into the spirit world, who have accepted the gospel and have turned their hearts and thoughts to their descendants on earth with the hope that their children will do the proxy work for them, while the children *represent* all those who turn their hearts and their labors in behalf of their dead progenitors in genealogical endeavors.

All the ordinances performed by proxy in behalf of the dead are carried out in the temples. But before the ordinances can be performed for a person, statistical information must be gathered identifying him or her as the one belonging to the ancestral pedigree. This is known as genealogical research.

The members of The Church of Jesus Christ of Latter-day Saints compile the name of each person, together with the dates and places of his or her birth, marriage, death and other pertinent information which is placed on specific genealogical forms and sent to the Genealogical Society. The forms are approved and sent to the temples where the proper baptisms, priesthood ordinations, endowments, temple marriages and other ordinances are performed by proxy, including sealing the person to his or her parents. Of this work, describing earthly and heavenly *counterparts*, Joseph Smith said:

> Now, the nature of this ordinance consists in the power of the Priesthood, by the revelation of Jesus Christ, wherein it is granted that whatsoever you bind on earth, shall be bound in heaven and whatsoever you loose on earth, shall be loosed in heaven. Or, in other words, taking a different view of the translation, whatsoever you record on earth, shall be recorded in heaven; for out of the books shall your dead be judged, according to their own works...according to the records they have kept concerning their dead. (D & C 128:8)

This sealing or binding power makes it possible for the joining of husbands and wives together, of sealing sons and daughters to their fathers and mothers in the spirit world the same as in mortal life, from generation to generation back to the patriarch Adam in preparation for the patriarchal form of the priesthood organization of the universe. "And as are the records on earth in relation to your dead which are truly made out, so also are the records in heaven," (D & C 128:14) the records on earth being a *counterpart* of those in heaven.

The genealogical records that are compiled on earth are a mere *symbol* of the vast record system that the Eternal Father must have to keep records of his countless offspring and their place of abode in the heavens. Before a person can become as God he will need to know how to keep the records of his own eternal family.

Of course none of those in the spirit world will be required to accept the temple ordinances performed in their behalf. They have their free agency, the same as anyone on earth, to choose or reject them. Also, no ordinance that is performed in the temples will be binding on the person for whom it is performed unless the person keeps the commandments and lives worthy of the sealing power of the Holy Spirit of Promise, the same as is the case with those who live in mortality.

Chapter Twelve

SYMBOLS RELATED TO THE MILLENNIUM AND RESURRECTION

The Earth to Return to a Paradisiacal Glory

The eternal lifespan of man begins as he is born a spirit child of the Father in pre-mortality, then falls from a spiritual state as *symbolized* by the fall of Adam and Eve, passes through mortality, is baptized by water and by fire, dies, passes through the spirit world, is resurrected, and finally enters one of the degrees of glory. The lifespan of the earth as a living creature *symbolically corresponds* to that of mankind. (*Discourses of Pratt*, p. 352-3) The earth was born as a creation of the Eternal Father, passed through the period of the Garden of Eden, fell, is going through a mortal state, and was baptized by the flood in the days of Noah. It will be baptized by fire at the beginning of the millennium, will pass through a paradisiacal state during the millennium, will die, will be resurrected, and finally it will become a celestialized globe.

The tenth Article of Faith of The Church of Jesus Christ of Latter-day Saints states that when Christ personally comes to reign on earth "that the earth will be renewed and receive its paradisiacal glory." During the millennial period the earth will be in a paradisiacal state as it was before the fall of Adam. Joseph Fielding Smith gave a brief description of the earth and its mortal and millennial states as being a *symbol or order* of the Telestial and Terrestrial glories:

> This earth is to be renewed and brought back to the condition in which it was before it was cursed through the fall of Adam. When Adam passed out of the Garden of Eden, then the earth

became a telestial world, and it is of that *order* today. I do not mean a telestial glory such as will be found in telestial worlds after their resurrection, but a telestial condition which has been from the days of Adam until now and will continue until Christ comes.

When Christ comes the earth will be changed and so will all upon its face. It will become a terrestrial world then and will so remain for 1,000 years; and all those who have lived a telestial law will be eliminated....The earth will be cleansed from its wickedness and pass into the terrestrial *order*. This will necessitate a change in the very elements of the earth, and also of its inhabitants; yet they will still be mortal. Those who belong to the terrestrial *order* will dwell upon the earth during this period. (*Doctrines of Salv.*, Vol. 1, pp. 85-86)

After the baptism of the earth with a flood, the Lord made a covenant with the people that He would never again flood the earth; and He sent the rainbow in the clouds as a *token* for a remembrance of this covenant. (Genesis 9:12-15) Ezekiel considered it another *symbol* in remembrance of Christ. "As the appearance of the bow that is in the cloud in the day of rain, so....this was the appearance of the *likeness* of the glory of the Lord." (Ezekiel 1:28) In addition to the rainbow, tradition, the Andean Indians in the 1500's stated that the ark was a *symbol* between God and man that there would never be another flood that would cover the earth and that the flood was an ancient *symbol* that there would be another destruction of the earth in the future which would be by fire. (*Liahona*, October, 1983, pp.52-53)

Baptism of the Earth by Fire

Orson Pratt described how the earth's future baptism by fire and the Holy Ghost is a *similitude* to that of man's:

The second ordinance instituted for the sanctification of the earth is that of fire and the Holy Ghost. The day will come when it shall burn as a oven, and all the proud, and all that do wickedly shall be as stubble; after which, the glory of God shall cover the earth, as the waters cover the deep. Here then is a baptism of fire first, then of the Holy Spirit. *As* man received the baptism of fire and the Holy Spirit through the laying on of the hands of a legal administrator, *so* the earth received the same, not through its own agency, but through the agencies ordained of God. *As* man becomes a new creature by being born again, first of water, then of the spirit, in the *same manner* the earth becomes a new earth by being born again of these cleansing and purifying elements. *As* man becomes a righteous man by the new birth, *so* the earth becomes a righteous earth through the same process. (*Journal,* Vol. 1, p. 331; see also 2 Peter 3:10; D & C 101:25)

This description should be interpreted more *symbolically* than literally inasmuch as the earth will continue to exist for another thousand years. However, it will change into a paradisiacal state. It will be purified by the presence of Christ "for he is *like* a refiners fire..." (Malachi 3:2-3) "and the hills melt, and the earth is burned at his presence..." (Nahum 1:5) "for the presence of the Lord shall be *as* the melting fire that burneth." (D & C 133:41)

The proud and wicked who are to be burned at Christ's coming are *represented* in the scriptures as "stubble." (D & C 64:24; Malachi 4:1; 3 Nephi 25:1) The dictionary describes stubble as that part of a plant that extends above the ground after the grain has been harvested. The Bible describes stubble as dry and easily blown before the wind, (Job 21:18; Nahum 1:10) and a poor building foundation material to withstand fire. (1 Corinthians 3:10-13) Thus those who have lost a strong foundation of faith in the gospel through pride, indifference and wickedness, and who are easily blown by the temptations of Satan are *symbolized* as stubble in the following scripture: "For behold, the day cometh, that shall burn as an oven; and all the proud, yea and all that do wickedly, shall be as stubble: and the day that cometh shall burn them up, saith the Lord of hosts that it shall leave them neither root nor branch." (Malachi 4:1)

However, the fire by which the wicked are to be burned will not be a hydrogen bomb nor flamethrowers nor other such earthly destroyers. Isaiah said that those who are to burn as stubble "shall not deliver themselves from the power of the flame..." yet "there shall not be a coal to warm at, nor fire to sit before it." (Isaiah 47:14) Thus fire is *symbolic* of whatever means by which the Lord and the angels will burn them. (D & C 29:9)

The Signs of Christ's Second Coming

Although Christ is to come in power and great glory (Isaiah 40:5) at the beginning of the millennium, he will come with an element of surprise in *similitude* "as a thief in the night." (2 Peter 3:10) However, there will be *signs* and *wonders* that will indicate that the time of His coming is close at hand, such as is illustrated in the parable of the "fig tree; when his branch is yet tender, and putteth forth leaves, ye know that summer is nigh...." Yet "of that day and hour knoweth no man." (Matthew 24:36) Among these *signs* are the *wonders* to be shown forth in the heavens and in the earth in the last days. "And they shall behold fire, and vapors of smoke...the sun shall be darkened, and the moon turned into blood, and the stars fall from heaven." (D & C 45:39-42; Joel 2:10, 30-31)

There are many who speculate that earthquakes and other catastrophes will pollute the atmosphere with fire and smoke which shall darken and redden the sun which is literally possible; but another interesting fulfillment of this prophecy is that these *signs* are in *similitude* of the apostate darkness that is covering the earth, and of the darkness and apostasy that shall cover the earth in the last days. Nephi predicted: "Behold all the nations of the Gentiles and also the Jews...behold, they will be drunken with iniquity and all manner of abominations." (2 Nephi 27:1-2) Inasmuch as the sun, moon and the stars are *symbols* of the celestial, terrestrial, and telestial glories, one can easily imagine that the evils of the world are *symbolically* darkening the light of the sun, that the governments of force and suppressed agency are causing the light from the moon to be turned to blood, and that apostates of The Church of Jesus Christ are leading other children of God away from the gospel of His kingdom and many are falling *as* stars fall from heaven.

The Death and Resurrection of the Earth

At the end of the millennium the earth must die, in *similitude* to the death of the Savior and that of mankind. It is to suffer a death in *similitude* to that "of many of the martyrs." (*Discourses of Pratt*, p. 370) It is to be sanctified and "prepared for celestial glory....Wherefore, it shall be quickened...and the righteous shall inherit it." (D & C 88:18, 26) The Lord said: "I say unto you that when the thousand years are ended, and men again begin to deny their God, then will I spare the earth but for a little season; And the end shall come, and the heaven and the earth shall be consumed and pass away, and there shall be a new heaven and a new earth." (D & C 29:22-23)

As with man, the final ordinance the earth is to undergo is that of its resurrection, (*Doctrines of Salv.*, Vol. 1, p. 74) after which it will become "a new heaven and a new earth....And I John saw the holy city, coming down out of heaven, prepared *as* a bride adorned for her husband." (Revelation 21:1-2) The bride is *symbolic* of Christ's Church on earth, which is to "be adorned as a bride for that day when thou (Christ) shall unveil the heavens..." (D & C 109:73-74) and of the Holy City as cited above.

The marriage of Christ and the Church that is to come *symbolizes* the union between Christ and the Church and the type of marriage relationship that there should be between husband and wife on earth. (Ephesians 5:22-32; *LDS Bible Dictionary*: "Marriage") Christ is called the Bridegroom in the scriptures wherein the people are warned to prepare for the Lord's coming. (D & C 133:10, 19)

In Christ's parable of the talents "the Kingdom of Heaven is *likened* unto ten virgins" who are warned that if they do not prepare themselves for the Bridegroom he will not know them at his coming. (Matthew 25:1-13) The *symbolic* meaning in this parable is that those on earth who do not prepare themselves for the kingdom of heaven will not be known or accepted by the Lord at his coming. The oil in the lamps *represented* the activities of those who prepared themselves through church service for the entrance into the wedding *symbolizing* those who prepare themselves through church service for entrance into the celestial kingdom. The foolish virgins expected entrance without their labors but were told that those who enter the wedding or celestial kingdom must do it "for yourselves...and the door was shut." (Matthew 25:9, 11)

An angel appeared to Saint John and said: "Come hither, I will show thee the bride, the Lamb's wife." The angel then *symbolically* described the Holy City of the celestialized earth because ordinary words cannot adequately describe how beautiful, grand, and wonderful the celestial glory will be for those who attain it. The angel described it as:

> Having the glory of God: and her light was like unto a stone...clear as crystal;

And had a wall great and high, and had twelve gates, and at the gates twelve angels, and names written thereon, which are the names of the twelve tribes of the children of Israel:...

And the wall of the city had twelve foundations, and in them the names of the twelve apostles of the Lamb....

And the building of the wall of it was of jasper: and the city was pure gold, like unto clear glass....

And I saw no temple therein: for the Lord God Almighty and the Lamb are the temple of it.

And the city had no need of the sun, neither of the moon, to shine in it: for the glory of God did lighten it, and the Lamb is the light thereof....

And there shall no wise enter into it any thing that defileth, neither whatsoever worketh abomination, or maketh a lie: but they which are written in the Lamb's book of life. (Revelation 21:9-27)

The Prophet Joseph Smith gave this description of a vision which he received:

I beheld the celestial kingdom of God, and the Glory thereof, whether in the body or out I cannot tell. I say the transcendent beauty of the gate through which the heirs of that kingdom will enter, which was *like unto* circling flames of fire; also the blazing throne of God, whereon was seated the Father and the Son. I saw the beautiful streets of that kingdom which had the *appearance* of being paved with gold. (*Teachings* p. 107)

The Resurrection of Mankind

At the end of the millennium all human beings that have lived on the earth who have not previously been resurrected shall be resurrected concurrent with the death and resurrection of the earth. Christ said that "All that are in the graves shall come forth." (John 5:28) "For as in Adam all die even so in Christ shall all be made alive." (1 Corinthians 15:22) Amulek said:

The spirit and the body shall be reunited again in its perfect form: both limb and joint shall be restored to its proper frame....

> This restoration shall come to all...and even there shall not so much as a hair of their heads be lost....
>
> This mortal body is raised to an immortal body...that they can die no more...thus the whole becoming spiritual and immortal, that they can see no more corruption. (Alma 11:43-45)

In a vision the Lord *symbolically* used a valley of dry bones to represent the dead and to illustrate to Ezekiel the process by which mankind is resurrected:

> The hand of the Lord...set me down in the midst of the valley which was full of bones....
>
> And, lo, they were very dry. Again he said unto me prophesy upon these bones...
>
> and as I prophesied, there was a noise, and behold a shaking, and the bones came together, bone to his bone.
>
> And when I beheld, lo, the sinews and the flesh came up upon them, and the skin covered them above: but there was no breath in them.
>
> So I prophesied as he commanded me, and the breath came into them, and they lived, and stood up upon their feet, an exceeding great army....
>
> And ye shall know that I am the Lord, when I have opened your graves,...
>
> O my people, and brought you up out of your graves, and shall put my spirit in you, and ye shall live...." (Ezekiel 37:1-14)

Special emphasis was made in the vision that the bones were very dry, *representing* that there was no blood in them. The resurrected bodies of flesh and bones will no longer contain blood. After the bones came together and the sinews, flesh and skin covered them, the breath or spirit of the Lord instead of blood came into them and they lived. The breath that entered the bones is *symbolic* of the spiritual material by which the bodies of resurrected beings will be quickened; it "is matter but it is more refined and pure and can only be seen with purer eyes." (*Teachings*, pp. 301-302) This is the reason that Paul said that "flesh and blood cannot inherit the Kingdom of God." (1 Corinthians 15:50) Flesh can, but blood will be replaced with a spiritual fluid when a person is resurrected.

The spirit of the resurrected body contains the pure, sanctified and glorified elements of immortality relating to immortality and to the Savior, "who shall change our vile body that it may be fashioned *like unto* his glorious body..." (Philippians 3:21) Flesh and blood *symbolizes* mortality, while flesh and bones *signifies* immortality in some of the scriptures.

The Differences of Bodies and Degrees in the Resurrection

But not all shall be resurrected with the same body or degree of glory. At the time of a person's death, he is placed in the spirit world in a state of happiness or misery according to which environment he is worthy to live in during his spirit world experience. (Alma 40:11-14) At the time he is resurrected, he is judged by the Lord as to which kingdom of glory he is entitled to inherit, based on how he has accepted and obeyed the commandments of God during his mortal probation and his sojourn in the spirit world.

People shall arise in immortality or, rather, be quickened by a portion of the particular kingdom of glory into which they are to enter at the time of their resurrection, be it as a celestial body or as a terrestrial body or as a telestial body (D & C 88:17-32; 76:70, 78) or with no glory whatsoever depending on their worthiness and capabilities: "For he who is not able to abide the law of a celestial kingdom cannot abide a celestial glory. And he who cannot abide the law of a terrestrial kingdom cannot abide a terrestrial glory. And he who cannot abide the law of a telestial kingdom cannot abide a telestial glory." (D & C 88:22-24)

Those who will not be able to abide even a telestial glory "must abide a kingdom which is not a kingdom of glory." (D & C 88:24) "Therefore they remain as though there had been no redemption made, except it be the loosing of the bands of death." (Alma 11:41) "They are they who are the sons of perdition of whom I (the Lord) say that it had been better for them never to have been born." (D & C 76:32) The type of body a person receives as he is resurrected will be of the nature of the kingdom of glory which he wil inherit and will there remain throughout eternity. So far as we know at present, he can never progress from one degree of glory to another. (*Doctrines of Salv.*, Vol. 2, pp. 22-23; D & C 132:16-17)

Since present earth life is *symbolic* of the telestial kingdom, and life during the millennium is *symbolic* of the terrestrial kingdom, (*Doctrines of Salv.*, Vol. 1, pp. 82-84) only those who attain celestial glory will enjoy an eternity of the fullness of joy *symbolized* by the utopia of peace and happiness everyone hopes to achieve. The righteous who gain celestial glory shall "shine forth as the sun in the kingdom of their Father," (Matthew 13:43) in *similitude* to the glory "of the sun, even the glory of God...whose glory of the sun of the firmament is written of as being *typical*." (D & C 76:70) In contrast, for those who gain the terrestrial and telestial glories there will be great remorse, for as Luke said: "There shall be weeping and gnashing of teeth, when ye shall see Abraham, and Isaac, and Jacob, and all the prophets, in the kingdom of God and you yourselves are thrust out." (Luke 13:28; see also Alma 42:1, 6; 41:4)

The Righteous to Reside as Eternal Parents With Heavenly Father

Those who gain the celestial kingdom will discover that the opportunities and capabilities to assimilate huge amounts of knowledge will be greatly accelerated and enlarged. They will

> ...reside in the presence of God on a globe *like* a sea of glass and fire, where all things for their glory are manifest, past, present, and future, and are continually before the Lord....
>
> And it will be *like* unto crystal and will be a Urim and Thummin to the inhabitants who dwell thereon, whereby all things pertaining to an inferior kingdom or all kingdoms of a lower order will be manifest....
>
> Then the white stone mentioned in Revelation 2:17, will become a Urim and Thummim to each individual who receives one, whereby, things pertaining to a higher of kingdoms will be made known.
>
> And a white stone is given to each of those who come into the celestial kingdom, whereon is a new name written, which no man knoweth except he that receiveth it. The new name is a key word. (D & C 130:6-11; 77:1; Revelation 15:2)

In *similitude* to the celestialized earth as a Urim and Thummim, individual revelatory instruments were used by Aaron "when he goeth in before the Lord" (Exodus 28:30; Leviticus 8:8); by several of the early prophets; (Deuteronomy 33:8, Abraham 3:4) and by the Prophet Joseph Smith to translate the *Book of Mormon* and other records. (D & C 10:1; 17:1)

The revelatory instruments used by Joseph Smith and the early prophets aided them in obtaining past, present, and future knowledge from on High in *a similar* way as the inheritors of celestial glory will gain knowledge through the white stone which "will be a Urim and Thummim to each individual who receives one,..." (D & C 130:10)

But those who attain celestial glory will not become a God quickly. Even with the assistance of the means *symbolized* by the white stone, it will take a great amount of time to become perfect. The more knowledge and intelligence a person receives in this life, through his diligence and obedience, the more advantageous it will be for him to attain this goal as the knowledge will rise with him in the resurrection. (D & C 130:18-19)

Some General Authorities suggest that no one will be perfect, as God is perfect, until he has attained that goal through continued diligence in the accumulation of knowledge and experience even after the resurrection. "That which is of God is light; and he that receiveth light and continueth in God, receiveth more light; and that light groweth brighter and brighter until the perfect day." (D & C 50:24) Other indications suggest that we will need enough light and knowledge to be as God before we are resurrected. Also, since it is necessary to be ordained into offices of the priesthood on earth a person who merits Godhood will probably be ordained to that position.

In the highest sense no one will be perfect until he attains his inheritance with the Father and lives the kind of life the Father lives, which is eternal life. Those who gain eternal life shall have "a continuation of the seeds forever and ever. Then shall they be Gods; because they have no end...." (D & C 132:19-20) A continuation of the seeds signifies that they will with their wives have spirit children the *same as* the Eternal Father has. (*Doctrines of Salv.*, Vol. 2, p. 68) No man can attain this position without a wife who has been sealed to him, and they both have attained exaltation. (D & C 131:2)

The highest degree is for the glorious expansion of the family as an eternal unit far beyond that experienced by a husband and wife and children while on earth, of which the earthly family is a *symbolic* preparation. Living and dwelling with the Eternal Father and the Son as an eternal and ever-increasing family was what John had in mind when he said: "And this is life eternal, that they might know thee the only true God and Jesus Christ whom thou has sent." (John 17:3) Those who come to know Him become like Him and will "receive their inheritance" and by becoming like him, "be made equal with him." (D & C 88:107) Equal, except that God the Father will continue to be the Father of all His posterity and those who will attain this inheritance will be part of the Father's dominions throughout eternity, maintaining the love, honor and parental respect of the eternal family relationship.

According to Elder Melvin J. Ballard, this process does not contradict the law of nature, nor is it difficult to understand:

> The nature of the offspring is determined by the nature of the substance that flows in the veins of the being. When blood flows in the veins of the being, the offspring will be what blood produces, which is tangible flesh and bones, but when that which flows in the veins is spirit matter, a substance which is more refined and pure and glorious than blood, the offspring of such beings will be spirit children. (*Sermons* pp. 239, 256)

This and the foregoing chapters have explained the grand and glorious realm of our Eternal Father and Mother in the universe. The chapters have explained the possibilities of our inheriting a partnership with Them as Their sons and daughters in celestial glory. God the Father provided the plans, means, and requirements under which we may attain this partnership. It is up to each person individually to determine for himself or herself as to what degree of salvation he or she wishes to attain, then to put forth the necessary effort to attain it. The following chapters highlight God's plan of salvation in its highest and purest form as is carried out in the House of the Lord.

Chapter Thirteen

CEREMONIES AND ORDINANCES
OF THE TEMPLES

The Temple as a Symbolic Beacon Toward Eternal Life

The *symbolic* culmination of the entire gospel of life and salvation is found in the temples of the Lord. It is a scale model of the universe (Nibley, *What a Temple*) Inside are taught the pure and basic principles of the gospel in condensed form. The temple is a *symbolic* beacon for all those who wish to gain eternal life.

The Salt Lake City temple of The Church of Jesus Christ of Latter-day Saints is the best-known of all the latter-day temples. The dedicatory inscription on the upper level of the east central tower of the temple reads: "HOLINESS TO THE LORD, THE HOUSE OF THE LORD." The first statement *symbolizes* the dedication of those who enter into a covenant in the temple to serve the Lord and their fellow beings; the second *represents* that the temples are the Lord's personal dwelling places or sanctuaries. Combined, in a broader sense they *represent* His church and kingdom on earth where people may go to receive instruction from and communicate, spiritually, with Jesus Christ. The Church would not be complete without temples nor has it been in the past dispensations of the gospel. Wherever God's chosen people have been on earth in sufficient numbers, temples have been a focal point of their activities. (D & C 124:39-40) The temple was not, however, used for general public worship, but was a place for the saints to perform sacred ordinances pertinent to the particular dispensation in which they lived and to receive revelation from the Lord. "And let them make me a sanctuary; that I may dwell among them." (Exodus 25:8) Temples are "sanctuaries specially dedicated for sacred rites and ceremonies

Figure 26: 3 east towers, 12 finials on each tower, HOUSE OF THE LORD inscription.

pertaining to exaltation in the Celestial Kingdom of God." (*Doctrines of Salv.*, Vol. 2, p. 231)

The Tabernacle of the congregation with its Ark of the covenant was used as a sanctuary while the Israelites traveled in the wilderness and afterward for many years. About 1000 B.C. Solomon built a magnificent temple which was destroyed in the year 586 B.C. It was replaced 70 years later under the inspiration and direction of the Lord and called the Temple of Zerubbabel, but wickedness among the people led to its destruction. Herod, about the time of Christ's advent, built a temple for the Jews as a political enticement, but the Jews at this time were not fully in accord with the Lord. Although the temple was visited by Christ, the ordinances were not as complete as in Solomon's Temple. (*House of Lord*, pp. 30-35) A temple, patterned after the temple of Soloman, was built on the American continent under the direction of Nephi and there was one in use when Christ visited the American Continent after His resurrection. (3 Nephi 11:1; 2 Nephi 5:16) Many edifices called temples have been uncovered among ancient archaeological ruins, but they were not sanctuaries of the Lord as was Solomon's temple. At best they were a distorted substitute; at worst they were sanctuaries of Satan where human sacrifices were held. In the present epoch there are many edifices called temples belonging to organizations other then The Church of Jesus Christ of Latter-day Saints. They are not temples in the sense that they are Holy Sanctuaries of the Lord.

There are many ways that a temple may be identified as a true temple or House of the Lord. One of these is in its construction. The Old

Figure 27:

Base on cornerstone.

Testament stressed the symbolic importance of cornerstones in temples, so much so that in some temples each cornerstone measured 17 to 69 feet long and 7 1/2 feet thick. (*Standard and Library Reference Bible*, by John A. Hertel, p. 8) Many of the present temples of The Church of Jesus Christ of Latter-day Saints have single large stones placed under each of the 4 corners called corner stones. The first one laid is called the chief cornerstone. During the construction of each new temple, the church conducts a cornerstone ceremony as has been done since the Nauvoo Temple. Much importance is placed on this ceremony because the temple and the four cornerstones are *symbolic* of the church organization and of the gospel plan of life and salvation, as Paul illustrated when he described the Lord's church: "Now therefore ye are no more strangers and foreigners, but fellow citizens with the saints, and of the household of God; and are built upon the foundation of the apostles and prophets, Jesus Christ himself being the chief cornerstone; in whom all the building fitly framed together groweth unto an holy temple in the Lord." (Ephesians 2:19-21)

In a discourse at the October, 1984 General Conference of The Church of Jesus Christ of Latter-day Saints, Elder Gordon B. Hinkley explained in some detail what the *representations* of the four basic cornerstones are and upon which the Church has been established by the Lord and "fitly framed together." He said that the first or chief cornerstone is the Lord Jesus Christ, whose name the Church bears. The second is the vision in which the Father and Son appeared to the prophet Joseph Smith. Included in this cornerstone would be the *rock* of revelation mentioned when the Lord told Peter that "upon this rock (the rock of revelation) I will build my church." (Matthew 16:17-18) The third cornerstone is the Book of Mormon. "It contains what has been described as the fifth gospel." Of course, the companion scriptures to this book are the *Bible*, *Doctrine & Covenants*, and the *Pearl of Great Price*. The fourth cornerstone is "the restoration to the earth of priesthood powers and authority," which is built upon apostles and prophets, with Jesus Christ himself being the chief cornerstone; (*Ensign*, November, 1984 pp. 50-52)

The Temple Ordinances and Ceremonies

The temples of the Lord are reserved for a place where advanced sacred ordinances, rites, and ceremonies can be performed in order to enable one to attain exaltation. Only members of The Church of Jesus Christ in good standing are permitted to enter the temples. Only they are able to understand the sacred ceremonies and appreciate their purpose. Elder John A. Widtsoe said:

> Many apostates have tried to reveal the ordinances of the House of the Lord. Some of their accounts form a fairly complete and correct story of the outward form of the temple service; but they are pitiful failures in making clear the eternal meaning of temple

worship and the exaltation of spirit that is awakened by the
understanding of that meaning. Such attempts are only words;
symbols without meaning.

Such attempted improper revelations of temple worship have
led in all ages to corruptions of temple ordinances...but they are
poor, lifeless imitations, *symbols* from which the meaning has
been wrested. (*Power From High,* pp. 43-44)

The temple ceremony is the least understood, yet the most important
of all the ordinances of the Lord's Church. Fewer than 50 percent of
Latter-day Saint youth are married in the temple, largely because their
parents, teachers and others do not attend often enough to understand
the real purpose and importance of the ceremony and to encourage
and teach the youth properly. Elder John A. Widtsoe, concurring in
a statement that "we should give more attention to preparing our young
people and some of the older people, for the work they are to do in
the temple," said: "It is not quite fair to let the young girl or young
man enter the temple unprepared, unwarned, if you choose, with no
explanation of the glorious possibilities of the first fine day in the
temple." (*U G & H,* Vol. 12, p. 64, April, 1921.)

This chapter is especially written for those who enter the temple
as a guide to help them better understand the deep meaning of the eternal
truths found in the temple ceremonies and what is permissible to teach
to their children and others. Most of the temple ceremony and
ordinances performed in the temple are not to be discussed outside
of the temple, but there are some things written about the temple
ceremony and ordinances by some of the General Authorities of the
Church and others which may be repeated. These items are in articles
published in church books or magazines. The following paragraphs
are limited for the most part to quotations from such articles or to the
four standard works of the Church. While reading and while in the
temple keep in mind that "To understand the meaning of temple worship,
it is necessary to understand the plan of salvation and its relation to
temple worship." (John A. Widtsoe, *Saviors,* p. 163; *U G & H,* Vol.
12; p. 54, April, 1921)

In order for a person to understand the ceremony and ordinances
of the temple, he or she must realize that almost everything being taught
is *symbolic* of the plan of salvation, the purpose of the principles of
the gospel, and of the methods by which God may bring to pass the

eternal exaltation of those who attend. According to David R. Roberts, a former officiator in the Salt Lake Temple:

> One person may explain or show a *symbol* to another,...but no man can reveal to another the sublime, deep inner meaning of those *symbols* presented in the House of the Lord, for it is an individual matter, and every soul must seek and obtain it for himself, and that alone, with God's help only. Nor can anyone acquire this knowledge outside the House of the Lord, for there he must go to commune with Him about these vital things. (*Power From High,* 1937, p. 48)

Sealing by Proxy

As was the case in Solomon's temple, a baptismal font resting on 12 oxen is located in the basement of some of the present Latter-day Saint temples. They are so located because of the *symbolism* of the baptized person being buried in the *likeness* of Christ's death and resurrection, (Romans 6:1-10) with the added *symbolism* that the baptismal fonts in the temples are only used for baptisms for the dead. The font "...was instituted as a *similitude* of the grave and was commanded to be in a place underneath where the living are wont to assemble to *show forth* the living and the dead, and that all things may have their *likeness*...that which is earthly *conforming* to that which is heavenly, as Paul hath declared." (D & C 128:13; 1 Corinthians 15:46-48) The baptismal fonts of ancient days were for baptism of the living only; the ones in the Latter-day Saint temples are used to baptize individuals standing as proxy for the dead, and such baptism are restricted to performance in temples only. (*House of Lord,* p. 87)

In the upper part of the temple are sealing rooms with an altar at the center. Here temple marriages are performed in which the couple is sealed for time and for all eternity. At the altar the couples pledge eternal love and mutual fidelity each for the other *symbolically* in the presence of "God and the Angels." (*Improvement Era*, August 1962, pp. 574, 598; *House of Lord,* p. 103) Of this ceremony Elder Widtsoe said: "The mere words of sealing may be easily spoken at the altars of the holy temples, but they are so full of meaning that any man with even a particle of imagination, who witnesses or participates in the sealing ordinance, must be overcome with the feeling of responsibility, and opportunity and enjoyment that it carries with it." (*U G & H,* Vol. 12, p. 56, April, 1951; *Saviors,* p. 164)

Children born to parents who have previously been sealed are "Born in the covenant" and are automatically sealed to their parents for eternity, conditional on their worthiness. Sometimes a couple that has been married outside of the temple will later decide to be sealed to each other in the temple for eternity. In the meantime, if children have been born to them, these children can be taken to the temple and sealed to their parents. If any of these children are dead, someone must stand in their place as proxy. Into the sealing rooms also go those who stand proxy for the deceased husband, wife, and children who did not have the opportunity to hear and accept the gospel while in this life. Here a man and woman by *proxy* are sealed for all eternity in behalf of the dead parents, and then other individuals acting as *proxies* are sealed to the parents in behalf of those who were the children of the couple during earth life. They are sealed together as a family unit, predicated upon their faithfulness in accepting the gospel and keeping the commandments of God. On these occasions the sealing room "is a fitting *symbol* of the actuality of communication between the dead and the living." (*House of Lord,* p. 191)

The Temple Endowment

In addition to the marriage ceremony, each man or woman must receive his or her "endowments" in order to be eligible for exaltation. Receiving an endowment is the act by which a person passes through the temple ceremony. In brief, Brigham Young gave a description of the endowment:

> Your endowment is to receive all those ordinances in the House of the Lord which are necessary for you after you have departed this life, to enable you to walk back to the presence of the Father, passing the angels who stand as sentinels, being enabled to give them the key words, the signs and tokens, pertaining to the holy Priesthood, and gain your eternal exaltation in spite of earth and hell. (*Discourses of Young,* p. 416)

Baptism is the ordinance permitting entrance into the celestial kingdom, but baptism is not the only ordinance required for exaltation in that kingdom. In the celestial glory there are three heavens or degrees.

No person can gain the highest (exaltation) without the ordinances of the temple. (*Doctrines of Salv.,* Vol. 2, p. 45; D & C 124:28-39)

The temple endowment involves two qualities—power and knowledge. First, quality: the individual receiving the endowment may actually be endowed with power from God: "I gave unto you a commandment that you should build a house, in the which house I design to endow those whom I have chosen with power from on high." (D & C 95:8; 110:9) According to Elder Widtsoe, power from on high is "Knowledge made alive and useful—that is intelligence; and intelligence is action. Our temple gives us power—a power based on enlarged knowledge and intelligence." (*Saviors,* p. 164; *U G & H,* Vol. 12, p. 55, April, 1921) Second quality: this power is based on enlarged knowledge and intelligence of a quality in *similitude* to God's own power. The endowment, therefore, is a means by which a person may become entitled to receive the highest powers of Godhood. It is also a course of instruction in the highest principles and ordinances of the gospel, in order that he or she might gain exaltation. Joseph Smith said:

> The main object was to build unto the Lord a house whereby He could reveal unto His people the ordinances of his house and the glories of His kingdom, and teach the people the way of salvation: for there are certain ordinances and principles that, when they are taught and practiced, must be done in a place or house built for that purpose. (*Teachings,* p. 308; D & C 124:40-41)

All that we receive of the gospel while on earth is given to us to help us develop and prepare ourselves for exaltation in the celestial glory. The temple endowment is the basic means by which the Father *symbolically* teaches his children on earth the steps they must follow. Elder Widtsoe said:

> The temple ordinances encompass the whole plan of salvation, as taught from time to time by the leaders of the church, and elucidate matters difficult of understanding. There is no warping or twisting in fitting the temple teachings into the great scheme of salvation. The philosophical completeness of the endowment is one of the great arguments for the veracity of temple ordinances. Moreover this completeness of survey and expounding of the gospel plan makes temple worship one of the most effective

methods of refreshing the memory concerning the whole structure of the gospel. (*U G & H,* Vol. 12, p. 58, April, 1921; *Saviors,* p. 166)

"God's laws governing the world are *patterned* after the Celestial world." (Louise Y. Robinson, General President of the Relief Society, *Improvement Era,* Vol. 39, pp. 214-216, April, 1936) The laws and ordinances of the gospel are to teach and train us for that glory. The temple covenants and ordinances are advanced symbolic representations to help us better understand the laws and ordinances of both this earth and the celestial kingdom. (*U G & H,* Vol. 12, p. 61, April, 1921; *Saviors,* p. 167) Elder Widtsoe continues:

> It is a series of *symbols* of vast realities, too vast for full understanding. Those who go through the Temple and come out feeling that the service is unbeautiful have been so occupied with the outward form as to fail to understand the inner meaning...
>
> No man or woman can come out of the temple endowed as he should be unless he has seen, beyond the *symbol*, the mighty realities for which the *symbols* stand.
>
> To the man or woman who goes through the temple with open eyes, heeding the *symbols* and the covenants, and making a steady, continuous effort to understand the full meaning, God speaks his word, and revelations come. The endowment is so richly *symbolic* that only a fool would attempt to describe it; it is so paced full of revelations to those who exercise their strength to seek and see, that no human words can explain or make clear the possibilities that reside in temple service. (*U G & H,* Vol. 12, pp. 61-63, April, 1921; *Saviors,* pp. 167-168)

The Modes and Methods of Endowment Instruction

As one goes to the temple he *symbolically* leaves the world of evil and strife and enters the abode of the Lord, and if he will study and be prayerfully attentive, he will in time gain most of what the Lord is teaching in the endowment. It does not come with the first visit but takes many trips through the temple. One of the advantages of proxy service for the dead is that a person may visit the temple often for continued instruction and inspiration. These instructions are given through several modes. Elder Widtsoe said:

The endowment and temple work as revealed by the Lord to the Prophet Joseph Smith fall clearly into four distinct parts: the preparatory ordinances; the giving of instructions by lectures and representations; covenants; and finally, tests of knowledge....The candidate for the temple service is prepared, as in earthly affairs, for work to be done. Once prepared, he is instructed in the things that he should know; when instructed, he covenants to use their imparted knowledge, and at once the new knowledge, which of itself is dead, leaps into living life. At last tests are given him, whereby those who are entitled to know may determine whether the man has properly learned the lesson....

How is all this accomplished? First by the spoken word, through lectures and conversations, just as we do in a classroom except with more elaborate care, then by appeal to the eye by *representations* by living moving beings; and by pictorial *representations* in the wonderfully decorated rooms, (or by moving pictures). Meanwhile the recipients themselves, the candidates for blessings engage actively in the temple service...with the progress of the course of instruction. (*U G & H,* Vol. 12, pp. 58-59, April, 1921; *Saviors,* pp. 166-167)

According to Elder James E. Talmage:

This course of instruction includes a recital of the most prominent events of the creative period, the condition of our first parents in the Garden of Eden, their disobedience and consequent expulsion from that blissful abode, their condition in the lone and dreary world when doomed to live by labor and sweat, the plan of redemption by which the great transgression may be atoned, the period of the great apostasy, the restoration of the gospel with all its ancient powers and privileges. The absolute and indispensable condition of personal purity and devotion to the right in present life and a strict compliance with Gospel requirements....

The ordinances of the endowment embody certain obligations on the part of the individual, such as covenant and promise to observe the law of strict virtue and chastity, to be charitable, benevolent, tolerant and pure; to devote both talent and material means to the spread of truth and the uplifting of the race; to maintain devotion to the cause of truth; and to seek in every way to contribute to the great preparation that the earth may be made ready to receive her King,—the Lord Jesus Christ. With the taking of each covenant and the assuming of each obligation a promised blessing is pronounced, contingent upon the faithful observance of the conditions. (*House of Lord*, pp. 99-100)

In the Salt Lake and in some of the older temples, the course of instruction is carried on as those attending pass from room to room. Elder Hugh B. Brown described the rooms briefly in an article in the Improvement Era:

The Garden Room in the temple is *symbolic* of the Garden of Eden which the Lord prepared for Adam and Eve.

The World Room in the temple is *symbolic* of the dreary and bleak world into which Adam and Eve were driven after they had partaken of the forbidden fruit of the tree of the knowledge of good and evil.

The Terrestrial Room in the temple *symbolizes* the second degree of glory.

The Celestial Room *symbolizes* the high degree of exaltation to which man may attain if he lives according to the saving principles of the gospel of Jesus Christ. (*Improvement Era*, August, 1962, pp. 570-575)

The Celestial Room is *symbolic* of the happiness and joy one will have in the celestial glory. ("House of the Lord," a Latter-day Saint film strip) (For a well detailed and descriptive use of the rooms see *House of Lord*, pp. 185-195)

Brigham Young said:

A great many of you have had your endowments, and you know what a vote with uplifted hands means.

It is a *sign* which you make in *token* of your covenant with God and with one another and it is for you to perform your vows. When you raise your hands to heaven and let them fall and then pass on with your covenants unfulfilled you will be cursed. (*Discourses of Young*, p. 396)

The Principles and Ordinances of the Temple

The Lord commanded the early saints to build a house unto Him and said that He commanded Moses to build a tabernacle that His "ordinances might be revealed:"

> And again, verily I say unto you, how shall your washings be acceptable unto me except ye perform them in a house which you have built to my name?...
>
> Therefore, verily I say unto you, that your anointings and your washings, and your baptisms for the dead, and your solemn assemblies...are ordained by the ordinance of my holy house which my people are always commanded to build unto my holy name. (D & C 124:37-40)

According to the *Funk & Wagnalls Company Dictionary of Folklore*, washing and cleansing as a *symbol* of purification is almost world wide. It also lists three taps or knocks as *representing* the act of penance; taking off sandals as *symbolic* of shaking the world from one's feet; and drawing back curtains as *symbolic* of admitting souls to paradise. (*Funk & Wagnalls Company*, pp. 1095-1096)

Two of the first *symbols* recorded in the scriptures were given by the Lord in the Garden of Eden. "So I drove out the man, and I placed at the east of the Garden of Eden cherubim and a flaming sword, which turned every way to keep the way of the tree of life." (Genesis 3:24, Moses 4:31) According to Webber, the flaming sword used at the expulsion of Adam and Eve is a *symbol* of the authority of god; (*Church Sym.*, p. 25) and according to Goldsmith, Cherubim is a term derived to *signify* angels. (*Life Symbols*, p. 414) The cherubim on the golden mercy seat of the tabernacle that the Lord had Moses build had wings, (Exodus 25:18-20) but their usage was entirely *symbolical* since angels do not have wings. "The cherubim on the Ark of the covenant were placed there as *symbolic* figures *representing* guardians whose wings protected the altar." (*Answers*, Vol. 1, p. 97) The wings on these and other Old Testament cherubim were a "*representation* of the power to move, to act, etc." (D & C 77:4) The veil of a temple is mentioned in the scriptures. It is often used as a *figurative* curtain that is drawn between mortal man and the realm of God. (Ether 3:6, 19; Exodus 26:33; D & C 67:10) It is the Lord's will that man should go to the temple often to "stand in holy places;

and prepare for the revelation which is to come when the veil of the covering of my temple in my tabernacle which hideth the earth, shall be taken off and all flesh shall see me together." (D & C 101:22-23)

When members of the church enter the temple to perform ordinances, they change from their everyday clothing to plain, clean white clothing. White is a *symbol* of purity so: "Here we will not only lay aside the clothing of the street, but the thoughts of the street, and will try not only to clothe our bodies in clean white linen but our minds in purity of thought." (Hugh B. Brown, *Temples of The Church of Latter-day Saints*, 1976, p. 16) Elder Widstoe said:

> In the temple all are dressed alike in white. White is the *symbol* of purity. No unclean person has the right to enter God's house. Besides, the uniform dress *symbolizes* that before God our Father in heaven all men are equal. The beggar and the banker, the learned and unlearned, the prince and the pauper sit side by side in the temple and are of equal importance if they live righteously before the Lord God, the Father of their spirits. (John A. Widtsoe, *Improvement Era*, October, 1962, p. 710)

When God found Adam and Eve naked in the Garden, he made "coats of skins, and clothed them." (Genesis 3:21; Moses 4:27) Herein the Lord *represented* that man and woman should strictly observe the high moral standards of Christ's church. After one has received his endowments in the temple, he is supposed to wear underclothes called garments. As with the coats of skins, the garments *symbolically* represent to the wearer that he should keep himself properly clothed and morally clean. Jesus Christ may have had this in mind when he said: "Behold I come as a thief. Blessed is he that watcheth and keepeth his garments lest he walk naked, and they see his shame." (Revelation 16:15) Both the garment and the endowment are *symbolic* of the great spiritual truths they *represent*. To understand their purpose and reap the benefits, the individual must look beyond the physical into the spiritual realms of the gospel, and he or she must continue to wear the garments while out of the temple.

For those who have been through the temple, the garment acts as a protection from evil and harm, but only insofar as it *symbolically* represents the power given by the endowment as one keeps the commandments of God. Similarly, the Star of David was worn in early

Judaism as an article of apparel as a *symbol* of magical or divine protection. (*Jewish Symbols,* Vol. 7, pp. 198-199) President Joseph F. Smith calls them the garments of the holy priesthood, (*Improvement Era*, Vol. 9, p. 813; *Temples*, 1945 ed., p. 239; 1968 ed., p. 276) but the garments, as such, do not convey any priesthood to the wearer nor do they have any priesthood powers. They are, however *symbolic* of the priesthood, and when anyone removes the garments or mutilates them or in any way disrespectfully uses them, he removes the power they *represent*. One should not only respect the garments but also live the kind of life they *symbolize*. *Symbolically*, according to Alma, one must have his "garments spotless" in order to be able "to sit down with Abraham, Isaac, and Jacob, and the holy prophets...in the kingdom of heaven to go no more out." (Alma 7:25) For those who will enter the "New Jerusalem...it is they whose garments are white through the blood of the lamb." (Ether 13:10) It is important that those who wear the temple garments do so properly and in accordance with instructions that come from the Prophet of the Church, or they will lose the blessings and benefits therefrom. President Joseph F. Smith said:

> The Lord has given unto us garments of the holy priesthood, and you know what that means. And yet, there are those of us who mutilate them, in order that we may follow the foolish, vain and (permit me to say) indecent practices of the world....Let us have the moral courage to stand against the opinions of fashion, and especially where fashion compels us to break a covenant and so commit a grievous sin. (*Improvement Era*, Vol. 9, p. 813; *Temples,* 1945 ed., p. 239; 1968 ed., p. 336)

In the Ark of the covenant, in Solomon's temple and in some of the present temples of The Church of Jesus Christ of Latter-day Saints, there is a room called the Holy of Holies. The Holy of Holies in a temple is commonly recognized by historians "As the residence of Deity, the high seat of authority, the door to the path of purification." (*Funk & Wagnalls Company,* p. 1096) According to Elder Talmage: "This room is reserved for the higher ordinances in the priesthood relating to the exaltation of both living and dead." (*House of Lord,* p. 194)

Chapter Fourteen

SYMBOLS AND REVELATION
IN AND ON THE TEMPLE

The Physical Symbols of the Salt Lake City Temple

The Salt Lake Temple is more unusual than other temples of the church in that inside and out are illustrations of numerous symbols. In fact, "The whole structure is designed to *symbolize* some of the great architectural work above." (Truman O. Angell, Salt Lake Temple architect, *Millennial Star*, May 5, 1874, p. 274) In other words, the Temple contains many symbols, both physical and spiritual, that *represent* aspects of God's plan of life and salvation, the organization and control of the universe, and man's relation thereto. The most obvious of them is a statue of the angel Moroni situated on top of the east center tower. It *symbolizes* the proclamation and restoration of the gospel of Jesus Christ, as recorded on the gold plates which Moroni delivered to the prophet Joseph Smith.

Figure 28: Angel Moroni statue.

140

These plates were translated into English by Joseph Smith and are now known as the *Book of Mormon*.

On the east and west ends of the temple are three tall spires or towers. (See Figure 26) Truman O. Angell, the Salt Lake Temple architect, said that the "spires and the twelve pinnacles (finials on each spire) are *emblematic* of the First Presidency, twelve Apostles, High Council, Bishops and Counselors and etc." (*Millennial Star*, May 5, 1874, p. 274) More particularly, the three taller eastern towers are *symbolic* of the Presidency of the Melchizedek Priesthood and the source of light, while the three shorter ones on the West are *symbolic* of the lessor or Aaronic Priesthood. Also, those on the east *represent* the church on the Eastern Hemisphere while those on the West *represent* the church in the Western Hemisphere. (*Temples,* 1945 ed., pp. 239-240)

Between the roof line and the top of each of these six towers is a set of twelve finials. Inasmuch as "the whole structure is designed to symbolize...," these unusual finials symbolize something particularly important. Different sources have suggested that they *represent* the twelve tribes of Israel, the twelve apostles, and the twelve high councilmen on both the eastern and western hemisphere. As to the twelve apostles, Christ Himself called twelve apostles in Palestine before His death and twelve in ancient America after his resurrection. Since the restoration of the gospel in these latter days there have been twelve apostles, some of whom were born in both hemispheres. There is no record of there being a separate high council called in the New Testament era, but the Lord established it in modern times "as the cornerstone of Zion." (D & C 124:131) On the top of each finial there is a sculptured flame *depicting* the light of the gospel that is being spread throughout the earth by those holding the authority of the priesthood, *represented* by the six towers on which they are located.

Wall Buttresses Containing the Earth, Moon and Sun Stones

Around the outside perimeter of the temple are fifty flat buttresses that project out from the walls and extend from the foundation to the top of the parapet above the roof line. The lowest sections of the buttresses consist of large pedestals that project out further than the buttresses above. Being larger, the pedestals *symbolize* that earth life is the foundation that prepares mankind for the kingdoms of glory. An earthstone is carved on all 50 pedestals. The original temple plans

Figure 29: Side of the temple showing pillars with sun stones and a 5-pointed star in the keystone over the window.

for the earthstones show them embossed with illustrations of a different portion of the earth on each side of the temple. These illustrations were to correspond with the four quarters of the earth, *signifying* that "The gospel has come for the whole earth." (Truman O. Angell, *Millennial Star*, May 5, 1874, p. 274)

On the next level above are carved stones depicting the moon in its many phases, called "moon stones." One side of the temple illustrates the first quarter of phases, the next side the second quarter, etc. Just under

Figure 30:

Pedestal with earth stone.

Figure 31:

Half moon phase.

the roof level, set in the same buttresses, are fully rounded carvings called "sun Stones," with a ring of triangular points surrounding the circular sun. (See also Figure 29) The points *represent* rays of light streaming from the sun, and from celestial glory. On most of the keystones for the windows, and in various other places, are beautiful relief engravings of five pointed stars. (See also Figure 29) The "earth stones" obviously *represent* our life on earth and the earth is *symbolic* of the telestial kingdom. The sun, moon and star stones are respectively *symbolic* of the celestial, terrestrial and telestial glories to which the souls of mankind will be assigned after resurrection according to the application they make of those things they learn and the covenants they make while in the temple (*Temples*, 1945 ed., p. 239)

Figure 32:

Sun stones with rays.

It would appear that there is a discrepancy in the placement of the earth stones at the lowest position on the buttresses, and the placement of some of the stars above the sun stones, inasmuch as the earth is to be celestialized and the stars *symbolize* the many abodes of the

Figure 33: Clouds with rays of light, 5-pointed stars, and circle combination.

telestial glory. However, at the present time the earth is mortal and as such *represents* the telestial glory. During the millennium it will *represent* the terrestrial, and after its resurrection it will become the celestial kingdom. At that time the telestial glory will have many and scattered abodes, as *symbolized* by the many and scattered stars on the temple.

The original temple plans show a "Saturn stone," with two circles around it, situated above the roofline at the top of each buttress. (Truman O. Angell, *Millennial Star,* May 5, 1874, p. 274). If the Saturn stones had been used, they would have *symbolized* a part of God's realm outside of or above the three degrees of glory, since they were to be placed at a level above the sun stones which *represent* the celestial glory and in the parapet above the rooms of the temple which *represent* man's progression from pre-earth life through earth life and into celestial glory. It is possible they were intended to *represent* Kolob, a star that Abraham saw in a vision which was very great and "nearest unto the throne of God." (Abraham 3:2-9) However, "Kolob" as a star was given power to govern planets of a lower order indicating that Kolob is a *symbol* of an order of the priesthood power of god in the universe more so than a physical star.

Another item that was on the original plans of the temple, but was omitted in the construction, is the square and compass. They are abbreviations of the full square and the double triangle described in the previous chapter. They were to have been placed at the side and toward the bottom of the oval windows. These windows were originally planed near the surface of the walls but were later set deep into the thick walls to show the solidity of the temple construction which made it impracticable to use the square and compass *symbols*.

The Miscellaneous Physical Symbols on the Salt Lake Temple

On the tower and above the roof line, on the east and west ends of the temple, are carved rows of squares with a circle set inside of each. (See Figure 33) As was explained in the previous chapter, the circle is *symbolic* of endless eternal life and perfection while the square, considered inferior to the circle, *represents* the earth and earth life. Combined, they would *symbolize* man's progression from mortal imperfection towards immortal perfection in God's plan of life and salvation, the guide for which is taught in the Lord's temples. (Matt. 5:48; 3 Nephi 12:48)

The keystones of the lower center windows of the east and west towers have inscribed on them "I am alpha and Omega." Alpha and Omega

Figure 34: Clasped hands in circle with rays, Alpha and Omega above.

are the first and last names of the Greek alphabet and are *"descriptive* names of the all-encompassing nature of Christ, being the first and the last, the beginning and the end." (Revelation 1:8-11; *LDS Bible Dictionary*, p. 606) Below these keystones, and on the escutcheons of the east and west double doors, are embossed emblems of the "Clasped Hands" (See also Figure 34) which are *symbolic* of the strong union

Figure 35: Clasped hands inside circle surrounded by olive wreath, symbolic doors and hinges.

of brotherly love characteristic of the Latter-day Saints; and by some of the New Testament Saints as the "right hand of fellowship." (*Temples*, 1945 ed., p. 136; Galatians 2:9) Directly above, at the top of the upper windows, is inscribed the symbol of the All-Seeing-Eye. Situated on the temple it *represents* the fact that "The Lord looketh from heaven;

Figure 36: All Seeing Eye in circle with veil-curtains and rays.

he beholdeth all the sons of men. From the place of his habitation he looketh upon all the inhabitants of the earth....Behold the eye of the Lord is upon them...." (Psalm 33:13-18) The eye is placed inside an oval circle that has points projecting outward and a curtain hangs over the eye. The circle with its rays *represents* God's heavenly abode while the curtain *symbolizes* the veil between the heavens and mankind. Near the top of the center buttresses of the east central tower are carved stones of embossed clouds with lines running downward (See Figure 33) that illustrate rays of light piercing through and streaming from the clouds, *symbolizing* gospel light dispelling the clouds of error, ignorance and superstition which has enshrouded the world. (*Temples* 1945 ed., p. 135; Truman O. Angell, LDS Temple pamphlet) Being located on the priesthood towers, these clouds with rays also *represent* the priesthood authority that is given the missionaries for them to carry the light of the gospel throughout the world.

In the upper level of the west central tower are embossed carvings of seven stars of Ursa Major or the Big Dipper, with the pointing stars directed toward the North Star. The location on the temple is significant because the inhabitants of the earth are *represented* by the earth stones below while their celestial goal is *symbolized* by the North star which is beyond the confines of the temple building and the reach of mankind in his mortal sphere; yet celestial glory is within reach of all who will

Figure 37: Big Dipper pointing to North Star.

look heavenward. Strengthening this concept is Nibley's statement that a temple is a scale model of the universe and that "as the pivot and pole of the universe the temple is also peculiarly tied to the North Star." (*What is a Temple*, pp. 230, 232)

There are four interpretations concerning the symbolic *representations* of the big Dipper on the temple. All four are similar but with interesting variations: (1) "To remind those in doubt concerning the true way that they should follow the path indicated by the priesthood." (*Temples*, 1968 ed., p. 131) (2) "That herein he will find an unfailing guide, as he or she travels the journey of life, which will safely guide them back to the Father's presence." (*Temples*, 1945 ed., p. 239) (3) "Moral, the lost may find themselves by the priesthood." (*House of Lord*, p. 145) (4) "Illustrates how the priesthood points men toward eternal life." (Truman O. Angell and the *Salt Lake Temple* pamphlet)

The Symbols on the East and West Doors

There are two pairs of large outside doors on the east and on the west ends of the temple, on which are inscribed several symbolic items. Each of the upper four of the six panels in each door contain stylized

Figure 38: East and west doors, Salt Lake Temple; 12-pointed star with beehive, circles of eternity, olive branch hinges with flower stars.

twelve-pointed stars surrounding a circle, the *symbolism* of which is explained among the miscellaneous symbols. They are a fancier version

Figure 39

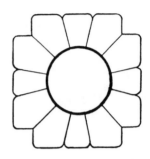

Figure 1

of the twelve pointed stars. In the
center of each panel, and on each of
the doorknobs, is an embossed
beehive with bees. (See also Figure
38) The beehive is commonly known
as an early LDS *symbol* of industry.
The church teaches industry and
thrift, and bees are industrious, functioning with almost perfect obedience
in a well executed organization.
However, the beehive symbolism goes
deeper than that. Before Utah became
a state the name of "Deseret" was

Figure 2

adopted by the territory because of its symbolic implications. When
the Jaredites left the tower of Babel and fled under the guidance of
the Lord to a promised land on the American continent, they carried
with them deseret, "which by interpretation is the honey bee." (Ether
2:1-3) Similarly, when Moses and the children of Israel fled from bondage in Egypt they were guided to a "land flowing with milk and honey."
(Exodus 3:8, 17) The Latter-day Saints *likewise* fled from their op-
pressors in Missouri and Illinois under the guidance of the Lord to
"a land of promise, a land flowing with milk and honey" that was promised to them as an inheritance which they named "Deseret." (D &
C 38:18-20) In each case the land that the Jaredites, Israelites and Mormons fled to became lands flowing with milk and honey. However,

Figure 40: Outside door knobs and escutcheon.

it wasn't without effort. Although the raw products were available, it required hard labor and the industry of the people to obtain the "milk and honey." Thus the beehive is a *symbol* of their past industry and the efforts of all who will be righteously industrious in the future.

The two lower panels of each door contains a series of symbols that point toward a insignia in the center containing the letter L which *represents* the Lord. (See also Figure 38) He said, "All things have

Figure 41: Lower panel of temple doors. Circle, vines, scroll and interlaced lettering representing House of the Lord.

their *likeness* and all things are created to *bear record* of me." (Moses 6:63) First, there is a triangle at each of the four corners of each panel. Second, there are several large circles *representing* eternity, everlasting life, perfection and eternal life. Inside each circle is a flourishing wreath of vines. Vines were frequently used in the *Bible*, Jewish writings, and the *Book of Mormon* as a *symbol* of Jewish and Christian churches, but more specifically of the spiritual life of Jesus Christ. (*LDS Bible Dictionary*) He said, "I am the vine and ye are the branches; He that abideth in me and I in him, the same bringeth forth much fruit." (John 15:1-8) As such, the vine *represents* the bringing forth of the fruit of the gospel that is taught in the temples to Christ's disciples who are *represented* by the branches. Inside the wreath is situated a scroll which *symbolizes* the power of the Lord when "at his great command the earth shall be rolled together as a scroll." (Mormon 5:23) And "the curtain of heaven be unfolded as a scroll is unfolded after it is rolled up, and the face of the Lord shall be unveiled" (D & C 88:95) in that "great day (of judgment) when ye shall be brought before the Lamb of God." (Mormon 9:2) First the principles of the gospel are taught to those who attend the temple, then the basis under which they shall be judged are set forth in the "House of the Lord."

Inside each scroll is a set of interwoven letters. (See Figures 38 & 41) A search in the BYU library, the LDS church historical library and other sources revealed nothing that the temple architects or early church leaders had left concerning the *symbolism* of the scroll or lettering. The large, stylized L apparently *represents* the Lord. The insignia in the center has the appearance of a foreign language letter. With the help of David Wright of the BYU Hebrew Department we were able to determine that it consisted of three letters: a T overlapping an H with an E at the top lacing them together forming the word THE. An O is laced over the L to the left and a not-so-obvious F is situated at the right of the T-H-E. The letter H also doubles for the word HOUSE. Thus the letters form THE HOUSE OF THE LORD. The O may have been laced onto the L for convenience, or it may *symbolize* the circle of eternity as it *symbolically* binds the House of the Lord together with the house of the Eternal Father in His celestial realm.

Extending from each of the eight hinges on the temple doors is a long stylized olive branch with leaves and blossoms (See Figure 38) Each blossom is in the form of a five-pointed star. Also at the top of each door escutcheon is an olive branch wreath. (See Figure 35) There are several references and parables in the scriptures wherein the olive tree *symbolically* refers to the House of Israel and the grafted branches *represent* the Israelites. (1 Nephi 10:14; D & C 101:44-62, etc.) Others relate to the temple and the activities therein. The two doors of Solomon's temple were of an olive tree. (1 Kings 6:31-33) The prophet Haggai spoke of the olive tree in connection with the blessings that the people would receive "from the day that the foundation of the Lord's temple was laid." (Haggai 2:15-19)

Section 88 of the *Doctrine and covenants* was designated by Joseph Smith as the "olive leaf...plucked from the tree of paradise...." (Heading, chapter 30; *History of Church,* Vol 1, p. 303) It is interesting to note that many of the principles and symbolic representations listed in Section 88 are basic to those taught in the temple, such as the book of names of the celestial world; the promise of eternal life; the light of the sun, moon and stars and the powers by which they were made; the light of God which giveth life to all things; the times, seasons and days given to man; laws governing those who will achieve celestial, terrestrial and telestial glories; to find God "knock and it shall be opened unto you;" the coming of the millennium, and the binding of Satan.

About half way up on the outside strips of the lower half of each escutcheon are four petal rosettes inside a circle and in the center below the shell is an eight petal rosette. (See Figure 40) Such rosettes were an outgrowth and variation of the four-sided square and the eight points of the interlaced squares, many of which are illustrated in Goodenough's books of symbols, especially volume 7.

On the temple door escutcheons and directly above each of the doorknobs are engraved a pair of stylized doors with large hinges. (See Figure 35) Since the door engravings are non-functional they *represent* something specific. Doors are a common *symbol* used in the scriptures to denote the means by which men and women gain access to Jesus Christ, our Eternal Father, and the celestial kingdom. Jesus said, "I am the door: by me if any man enter in, he shall be saved, and shall go in and out, and find pasture." (John 10:9) The door engraving and this scripture has greater symbolic significance if we consider that the temple is the Lord's House, that we must enter it to gain access unto the celestial kingdom and that we can go in and out of the temple doors to feed on pasture on God's plan of salvation and to receive the ordinances of celestial glory.

Embossed on the knobs and escutcheons of the temple doors, and on the west end of the celestial room, there are scallop-type shells.

(See Figure 40) Drawing from Jewish and other ancient sources, Irwin Goodenough described a number of ideas concerning these shells which are quite representative of gospel principles and that *symbolically* point towards Jesus Christ and the birth, death and resurrection of mankind, as does baptism. Among these are the concept that the shell is a *symbol* of a new life born of water and the spirit; new life and birth; immortality in the form of rebirth; the deceased is himself born into divine life; new and divine life; divine birth; and light. Additional signification was given to the shells, in as much as the major emphasis was to locate then over the doors and windows of synagogues, tombs, shrines, and on lamps. This is significant because doors *represent* the entrance into Christ's church, immortality and the celestial kingdom; while lamps *represent* Christ as the source of light.

The Temples as Places for Revelation

The Lord's true temples are a place and symbol of many things: they are a house of the Lord, a place of revelation, and a connecting link between the heavens and the earth. Brigham Young said: "We build temples because there is not a house on the face of the earth that has been reared to God's name which will anywise compare with his character, and that he can consistently call his house." He requires his servants to build him a house that he can come to where he can make known his will. (*Discourses of Young*, pp. 393-394) Of the temples the Lord said: "Yea, and my presence shall be there, for I will come into it, and all the pure in heart that shall come into it shall see God; but if it be defiled I will not come into it, and my glory shall not be there; for I will not come unto unholy temples. (D & C 97:16-17)

Of revelation in the temples Elder Widtsoe said:

> It is a great promise that to the temples God will come, and that in them man shall see God. What does this promised communion mean? Does it mean that once in a while...the pure in heart may see God there; or does it mean the larger thing, that the pure in heart who go unto the temples may, there, by the spirit of God, always have a rich communion with God? I think that this is what it means to me and to you and to most of us. We have gone into these holy houses, with our minds freed from the ordinary earthly cares and have literally felt the presence

of God....A temple is a place of revelation. (*U G & H,* Vol. 12, p. 56, April, 1921; *Saviors,* p. 164)

According to Elder Melvin J. Ballard, prayers are answered in the temple, and a person may have the guiding help needed in the problems of life both spiritually and temporally:

> We are in need of spiritual guidance today as never before. The wisdom of the Lord to solve our temporal problems is needed by our people....I commend this to you as a way to solve your problems. Study it out in your own minds, reach a conclusion, and then go to the Lord with it and he will give you an answer, by that inward burning, and if you don't get your answer I will tell you where to go—go to the House of the Lord,...and in the silent moments, the answer will come. (*Saviors,* p. 200)

Elder John A. Widtsoe adds:

> I believe that the busy person on the farm, in the shop, in the office, or in the household, who has his worries and troubles, can solve his problems better and more quickly in the house of the Lord than anywhere else. If he will leave his problems behind and in the temple work for himself and for his dead, he will confer a mighty blessing upon those who have gone before, and quite as large a blessing will come to him, for at the most unexpected moments, in or out of the temple will come to him, as a revelation, the solution of the problems that vex his life. That is the gift that comes to those who enter the temple properly because it is a place where revelations may be expected. I bear you my personal testimony that this is so. (*U G & H,* Vol. 12, p. 63, April, 1921; *Saviors,* p. 168)

According to Elder Joseph Fielding Smith, the Endowment is a protection for this life as well as an ordinance of exaltation for life hereafter. The greater protection, of course, will be spiritual protection against the power of Satan:

> If we go into the temple, we raise our hands and covenant that we will serve the Lord and observe his commandments and keep ourselves unspotted from the world. If we realize what we are doing, then the endowment will be a protection to us all our

lives—a protection which a man who does not go to the temple does not have....

This protection is what these ceremonies are for in part. They save us now and they exalt us hereafter if we will honor them. (*Doctrines of Salv.,* Vol. 2, pp. 252-253)

There are, however many Latter-day Saints who do not understand that certain blessings are conditioned upon their genealogical activities and temple attendance as well as keeping all the covenants they make while attending the temple ceremonies. "And it shall come to pass, that if you build a house unto my name, and do not do the things that I say, I will not perform the oath which I make unto you, neither fulfill the promises which ye expect at my hands, saith the Lord." (D & C 124:47) All of the latter-day prophets have asked the members of the church to do temple and genealogical work for the dead. The Prophet Joseph Smith said, "The greatest responsibility in this world that God has laid upon us is to seek after our dead." (*Teachings*, p. 356)

There are many who feel that they are too busy and active in the quorums or auxiliary organizations of the church to take time out for temple activity. But there is not a service in the church that would not be better understood and better magnified if the individual called to that office would diligently attend the temple. According to the Lord, this diligence is one of the great purposes of the temple:

> Verily I say unto you, that it is my will that a house should be built unto me in the land of Zion like unto the pattern which I have given you....
>
> For a place of thanksgiving for all saints and for a place of instruction for all those who are called to the work of the ministry in all their several callings and offices;...
>
> That they may be perfected in the understanding of their ministry, in theory and in principle, and in doctrine, in all things pertaining to the kingdom of God on the earth, the keys of which kingdom have been conferred upon you. (D & C 97:10, 13, 14)

Inspiration from the influence of temple activity is needed in order to help keep husband and wife together. The many problems and activities that daily confront parents and their families are more easily solved and managed under the spiritual influence from temple attendance while the strength and power received there will help combat the influence of Satan. In the temples young married couples gain the strength to give them a better start in life and to rear their children properly, while to the older couples it gives the strength to keep their marriage intact and to endure to the end. The Prophet Joseph Smith said, "You need an endowment, brethren, in order that you may be prepared and able to overcome all things." (*Teachings,* p. 91)

Spiritual Experiences Available in the Temple

Many of those who become actively engaged in temple and genealogical work have very unusual and faith promoting experiences. "All men and women who go into these houses may get an individual testimony for themselves that these things are from God." (Melvin J. Ballard, *Saviors,* p. 200) There are many ways in which a testimony of temple work will come often in a subtle manner. Many persons have received experiences similar to one related by Edward J. Wood, President of the Alberta, Canada Temple. He told how during a caravan visit to the temple, an elderly woman was in the temple to do work for herself and to have the work performed for her husband, and then to be sealed to her husband, and their children sealed to them. Following is a summary of the experience he had during this sealing:

> The sealing room was filled with neighbors and friends who wished to do the old lady honor. As I held the sheet in my hand to seal the two sons whose birth and death, etc., were fully filled out by the old lady, (their mother) I was impressed to ask her if these two sons were the only children she had, and she said: "Yes." I then proceeded to seal these sons, when I heard a voice behind me, as I thought, saying "I am her child." I then stopped and asked again: Are you sure you never had any other children?" She answered as before, but with some hesitation "Yes, Brother Wood, the record is right." But I felt sure there was a feeling of doubt in the room, and as I was again about to proceed, the voice again spoke to me with greater emphasis, saying, "I am her daughter." I looked around and into the faces of all who witnessed this wonderful manifestation, and then I spoke as kindly as possible to the old lady, saying "Surely grandmother, you had a daughter, didn't you?" She then broke into tears and asked that

all be seated and said she hoped we would forgive her, as she had had a little girl in her early married life and then a lapse of several years before she had the two boys in their order, and that in her great anxiety to have her work and that of her husband, and making of the sheet, to have her children sealed while on this, her first visit to a temple she had overlooked recording the name of the little girl who had died. (*U G & H,* Vol. 23, pp. 149-150; *Temples,* 1968 ed., p. 166; 1945 ed., p. 171)

As the author of this book I would like to add my testimony that faith-promoting experiences may be received in connection with temple and genealogical activity. I quote this example from my personal history:

My wife and I had placed a deposit to buy a lot in order to build a much-needed home. We were attending the temple once a week at the time, and during one of these weekly visits I had a dark, strange feeling that we should not build the house. But our needs offset the feelings so I pushed the thoughts aside. The following week the same dark feelings occurred, but seeing no particular reason for not building I set them aside again. When even darker feelings came the third week, I began to realize that they were more than mere misgivings about building a new home. While I was sitting during an inactive period, I decided someone from the spirit world was trying to tell me that we should not build a house.

At that moment I had a very unusual spiritual experience. Some kind of power or influence seemed to come over me to the extent that I had a sensation of hearing a sound like the rushing of waters, which reminded me of those recorded in *Doctrine and Covenants* 110:3. This power seemed to turn my head to look upwards where I expected to see an angel, but as I started to respond I became aware of the people sitting around me and I looked to see if they had heard or seen anything. They hadn't, and my thoughts returned to normal. The experience left me with the very strong feeling that we should not build. We went back to the lot owner, explained our situation, and he released us from our offer on the lot.

Six months later, my wife had the opportunity to manage the local railroad station in Bountiful, Utah, into which we moved. This move placed us in another ward in the church, where I was called as the ward Sunday School genealogical teacher. Looking for some teaching aids, I went into the old vault of the chapel. There I opened an old Centerville, Utah record book and discovered an 1854 tithing record of my second great grandfather. This was a big surprise because I had been informed that he never reached Utah—I'd been given to understand that he died while crossing the plains. After searching further, I found some 1851 rebaptism records, among which were listed his and his wife's parents.

Two or three years earlier I had hired a researcher in England to search the parish records of Clitheroe, the city from which my greatgrandfather had immigrated. The Clitheroe records listed a man and wife with the exact names as my great grandparents who were married at about the correct date, but with different parents than were listed in the Centerville records. As a result, I had accepted the researcher's findings of incorrect parents and I had been researching the wrong ancestral lines.

From the records I found in the vault, I was able to redirect my research to the proper lines. If we had built the house as we planned, we would never have moved into the ward where the records were found, and I and other members of the family would have continued researching the wrong ancestral lines. The old ward records were shortly sent to the Church Historian's Office in Salt Lake City where no one would have ever found the proper lines for my great grandparents. Certainly one or more of my dead ancestors who had accepted the gospel in the spirit world was directing me to those records.

The Holy Temples are earthly *symbols* of the heavenly kingdom of God, while man himself *symbolized* as a temple *represents* the pure type of a person he must become in order to inherit celestial glory. "Know ye not that ye are the temple of God, and that the spirit of God dwelleth in you? If any man defile the temple of God, him shall God destroy: for the temple of God is holy, which temple ye are." (1 Corinthians 3:16, 17) Those who keep their personal temples clean and pure from unholy influences may go to the temple of God and receive of God's bounteous blessings, but if they defile it, those blessings are withdrawn. If one's own body is clean and pure, it becomes a temple of righteousness where the spirit of the Lord may dwell but, like the temple God, the spirit of the Lord cannot dwell in an unclean tabernacle, in *similitude* that no unclean thing can enter the celestial glory. "The elements are the tabernacles of God; yea, man is the tabernacle of God, even temples; and whatsoever temple is defiled, God shall destroy that temple." (D & C 93:35; 97:17)

Symbols indirectly affect everyone. They can become a direct and worthwhile means of better understanding God's plan of life and salvation. They can be used to better understand the scriptures and to find the eternal truths that God has taught from Adam and the early prophets until the present. Accepting these truths into one's life will help lead one back into the Kingdom of God.

According to the parable of the one sheep out of the hundred that strayed, the Lord does not wish that one soul should be lost or destroyed. Rather he said, "For behold, this is my work and my glory—to bring to pass the immortality and eternal life of man." (Moses 1:39) It is the Eternal Father's and Mother's desire that every one of their spirit children return to them and become exalted as sons and daughters in Their celestial family.

Chapter Fifteen

EXPANDING HORIZONS

Alpha and Omega, an Emblem of Jesus Christ

Mention is made in chapter fourteen about the term "I am Alpha and Omega" as being the first and last letters of the Greek Alphabet and as descriptive names of Jesus Christ. The Bible uses the term Alpha and Omega to denote the Lord as "The Almighty." He said, "I am the first, and I am the last" (Isaiah 44:6). To the Nephites He said, "I am the light and the life of the world. I am Alpha and Omega...," and to the early Latter-day Saints He added, "Thus saith the Lord your God, even Jesus Christ, the Great I AM, Alpha and Omega, the beginning and the end...." (D&C 38:1; 39:1; Exodus 3:14). The terms "The Great I AM" and "Alpha and Omega" symbolize the Lord's course as one eternal round, the same today, yesterday, and forever (D&C 35:1).

An early first letter of the Greek Alphabet was shown as an Λ, the same as the first letter of the present English Alphabet, but the last letter of the Greek Alphabet was usually shown as Ω. Some encyclopedias of religion state that they were often shown on tombstones, monuments, mosaics, vases, lamps, etc. as ΛΩ to *represent* Jesus Christ as Alpha and Omega.

In later centuries a keystone at the crown of the Omega arch sometimes replaced the Λ, but such is logical considering that various definitions of a keystone are listed as: Locking other pieces in place, binding the whole, a basic *emblem* of doctrine, and a part or force on which associated things depend for support; all attributes of Jesus Christ. Often the words Alpha and Omega were inscribed on the keystone, but since Christ is the cornerstone of His church the *symbolism* remains the same in the Omega arch and the keystone, with or without the wording.

Alpha and Omega on LDS Buildings

The keystone bearing the inscription I AM ALPHA AND OMEGA is in the center of the arched symbol over the window openings of the Salt Lake Temple, but close examination reveals that the half circle extending down from each side of the keystone is situated on the surface of the window arch stones, thus forming a purely decorative symbol.

Figure 42: Alpha and Omega symbol
Salt Lake Temple

Figure 43: Alpha and Omega symbol
Manti Temple

The Alpha and Omega symbol as placed over the window openings of the Manti Temple represents Christ although the keystone is without the wording.

*Figure 44: Symbols on Logan
tabernacle tower*

There is an Alpha and Omega symbol located on each of the four sides of a tower on the roof of the Logan LDS tabernacle. Each Omega symbol surrounds the upper half of a circle in which is a five-pointed star called the Star of the East and the Star of Bethlehem which symbolized Divine guidance (see p. 31).

Figure 45: Face of Logan tabernacle

Also on the front face of the tabernacle there is an Omega symbol wherein the interlace triangles or Star of David is inside the circle and a stubby equal-arms cross is inside the star; the first a divine symbol, the latter a worldly one (see pp. 28, 33-34).

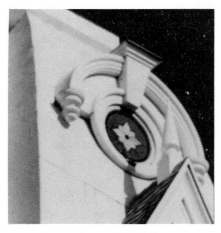

Figure 46: Assembly Hall tower

On each of the four sides of the tower on the roof of the Assembly Hall, on Temple Square in Salt Lake City, is an Alpha and Omega sign in which the keystone of the arch extends down into the circle, thus locking them together. This may have been done for ornamental purposes only, but this could *represent* interlocking Christ together with the never-ending universe represented by the circle. Inside each circle are two four-petal rosettes overlapping each other, which are decorative substitutes for interlaced squares signifying man's regeneration through the gospel principles and ordinances (see p. 30).

Separately, Alpha is listed in various dictionaries and encyclopedias as *signifying* the first letter of the Greek (eastern) alphabet, hence the first or beginning, specifically the chief, first in order of brightness, and the first-born in spirit. Omega is listed as the last letter of the Greek alphabet to denote Christ which is final, the end, the goal in all of creation. Combined they are described as the beginning and ending of all things, the chief of the whole, the all-encompassing nature of Jesus Christ, His high status in the Godhead, and the comprehensiveness of God; implying that He includes all that can be.

The Manti Temple Door Hardware

J. E. Circlot, in *A Dictionary of Symbols,* said that an Omega is similar to a torch. Some dictionaries describe a torch as anything considered as a source of enlightenment, inspiration, and knowledge. There is a formal design extending out of each side of a circle in the center of the door hinges of the Manti Temple which appears very much like a stylized

Figure 47: Manti door-hinge sketch

torch. There are six black dots on the stem of each torch representing the six days of the week, of creation, etc. (see pp. 34, 55). On the top of the stem is a cup with a dark band around the lower half with six light dots on each side which would form twelve on a full band. Above the band are four elongated shapes resembling a flame, which *symbolizes* purification, spiritual power, and a "means of devouring all things to return them to original unity." (J. C. Cooper, *Traditional Symbols,* p. 67.) If the two halves of the hinge were brought together, a circle would be formed with twelve sections surrounding a solid circle (similar to figures 1, 2 and 9). Twelve represents many things such as apostles, tribes, gates and foundations of the City of Zion (see pp. 22-23).

A common Egyptian symbol consisted of a square that turned the fourth side into an angle, leaving the square unclosed ⊓. It symbolized building (*Myth and Symbol,* p. 257). On the Manti Temple hinges, one of these designs is on each side of the torch stems. A full square *represents* building upright on a strong foundation, while an angle is an abbreviation of it (see pp. 29 and 35).

Some of the symbols inscribed on the door hardware of the Manti Temple are described by Dr. Hugh W. Nibley in an interesting article that he wrote for a book published by the Manti Temple Centennial Committee for their 100th-year anniversary celebration (*The Manti Temple,* pp. 34-36). He writes that the *symbolic* inscriptions on the hardware are Egyptian and believes they were designed by his Great Grandfather, John Patrick Reid, who worked on the temple. The article identified clusters of three discs ⋰ on the temple door knobs and push plates as representing the Egyptian idiogram KhW, designating bargains or agreements among people. On the doorknobs is a stylized L, and on both the knobs and escutcheons are full-circle rings of vines, two of which have circle 0's laced on them in the same manner as the L

Figure 48: Manti Temple door knob

(representing the Lord) of the interlaced lettering in the Salt Lake Temple door scroll (see figure 41). Vines are symbolic of the spiritual

life of Jesus Christ and the bringing forth of His gospel that is taught in The Church of Jesus Christ of Latter-day Saints. The circle is symbolic of everlasting life, perfection, and divinity. By lacing the circles onto the vines, the symbolism of both the circle and the vines are tied together in God's universe (see pp. 28, 29, 153).

Some doors originally had push-plates that were on large double doors in the entrance to the Manti Temple (since removed). Dr. Nibley says that the water jugs inscribed on them have a *meaning* of both heart or mind and unity or joining together, while the flowers growing from the jugs are *representations* of birth, sunrise, resurrection, and the eternal circle of life (*The Manti Temple,* p. 35). The blossoms themselves form actual symbols since they are composed of specific three round discs on the end of a stem, or geometric designs with seven, eight

Figure 49: Push-plate sketch

or twelve petals on each and a definite circle in the center. Placed vertically on each side and in the center section of each door plate is inscribed a row of X's. The three discs are apparently a decorative form of a triangle and would have the same meaning, such as the Godhead, birth, life and death, and man's rebirth by water, spirit and blood (see pp. 31-32). The seven-petaled flower *represents* the days of creation and of the week, and seven full ears for years of plenty and seven thin ears for years of famine. Eight sometimes *signified* man's regeneration and the basic principles of the gospel typified by the eight-petaled flowers while those with twelve points would be the same as the circle with twelve sections on the door hinges. Each of the blossoms has a circle in the center *representing* the no beginning nor ending of man's existence in the universe. The X's *represent* merging of the physical and spiritual aspects of mankind. (For more details, see pp. 23, 30, 31, 36, 37.)

Symbolic Flowers, Rosettes, and Designs in Temples

There are numerous symbolic designs in the Manti, St. George, and Salt Lake Temples. The greater emphasis of this section is for the reader to gain an insight into the types of symbols listed instead of duplicating many descriptions used in the foregoing and following sections.

There are glass panels in the double doors situated in the Celestial Room of the Manti Temple, each of which is etched with a jug and a flowering plant with blossoms stylized so as to indicate symbolic designs similar to the jug and flowering plant on the push-plates on the doors. Each blossom is shaped differently, with either three, four, five or seven petals and a circle in the center of each. Some leaves are in three- or six-pointed designs. The plant therefore represented the Godhead, the four corners of the earth, the Star of the East, and the seven times Joshua and his army marched around the walls of Jericho (see pp. 29, 31, 32, 39). The blossoms often resembled roses and were called rosettes (see pp. 40, 154). They were originally ornamental substitutes for the particular geometric design they replaced.

At the bottom of a stairway, the corner post has circles with eight petals in each plus some plain circles below. The corner post of another stairway has an octagon cubicle at the top with a set of circles on each of the eight sides. Further down is an eight-petal rosette inside a circle and below this is a blunt-corner square. On each side of a square knob of the stair-railing posts is a circle with two sets of four-petal designs overlacing each other, thus forming a set of interlaced squares. Also in the center of each pair of double doors are overlapping four-petal rosettes set inside a square which is set inside a circle. Next to the top of some of the columnar posts are square rosettes with a petal at each corner and smaller petals between, thus forming interlaced squares. Another column shows squares with X's inside the circles with twelve knobs in each. In the Terrestrial Room of the temple there are the original white wooden benches that were used almost 100 years ago. The ends of each bench are carved with eight-pointed rosettes surrounded by a circle, and with another circle in the center. Carved on each side of the base of columnar posts in the room, squares are placed with overlapping four-petal rosettes inside. Each of the circles symbolize perfection, infinity, eternal life, and without beginning or end. The squares *represent* the earth's existence with the principles of the gospel guiding man in his sojourn on earth. The X's represent the merging of the spiritual aspects of man's life, represented by the circle, with the worldly aspects as represented by the square (see pp. 28-30, 36).

There is a small room off the Celestial Room, in the Manti Temple, that was used for a Holy of Holies until the time the Salt Lake Temple was completed. The walls and ceilings are literally covered with symbolic designs. There are rows of plain circles, some with eight sections inside. There are squares with four-petal rosettes in each, and blunt-end crosses with circles inside. At first glance the stylized designs, in the upper half of the room, appear as flowering vines, but a closer examination reveals that the stylized blossoms on them are shaped more like stars with four, five, or eight points than blossoms or flowers.

In the St. George Temple there was originally a row of alternate five-pointed stars and bulky, blunt-pointed crosses situated on a cornice between the walls and ceiling of some of the rooms and in the priesthood assembly hall upstairs. The blunt crosses are almost identical to the crosses in the center of the Omega design on the face of the Logan Tabernacle (see figure 45). The temple was remodeled a few years ago but some of the rows of stars and crosses are still there to be viewed. They are appropriate because five-pointed stars point to the coming of Jesus Christ and *represent* His divine guidance while the cross represents His dealings with mankind on earth (see pp. 28, 31).

Popular Use of Flowers, Rosettes and Other Designs

Flowers and vines in stylized forms became very popular in many areas as substitutes for the geometric and other symbols they represented. Although they were used mostly for decorative purposes, they usually were situated in places where symbolic representation would be proper and expected, such as tombs and church buildings. Even those in the Manti, St. George, and Salt Lake Temples are situated in or near the celestial rooms.

In his book, *Roman Sources of Christian Art,* Emersen H. Swift has a photo of a large relief in the soffit of the Arch of Titus in Rome, 81 A.D. It shows dozens of squares. Inside the squares are rosettes in relief with six, seven, or eight petals on each one. In the center of each rosette is a circle divided into four, six or eight divisions. (See pp. 22-37 for meanings.)

Vines and squares, with very similar rosettes in each, were used extensively on some of the ceilings of the J. Paul Getty Museum in Malibu, California. The buildings were finished in 1974 and house hundreds of Roman antiquities, European decorative items, and other collections Mr. Getty gathered in earlier years. The museum building is a replica of the Villa di Papri at Herculaneum, Italy, which was destroyed in the eruption of Mount Vesuvius in 79 A.D. The rosettes on the ceilings are copies from extant models in Rome. The following details are from photographs furnished by the museum and are used in this chapter by their permission.

The rosettes, precisely designed with five, six, seven, eight, and twelve petals on each, were originally ornamental substitutes for the particular geometric design they replaced. Some of them consist of six prominent petals with six smaller ones between them, thus forming overlapping six-pointed interlaced triangles. In the center of each rosette is a raised circular center. Some are plain, others have three, four, five, or six divisions. Some of the centers have a triangle or square inside.

J. C. Cooper, in *An Illustrated Encyclopedia of Traditional Symbols,* p. 141, states that the four-petaled rose or rosette "depicts the four-square division of the cosmos; the five-petaled is the microcosm with the six-petaled as the mocrocosm." The rosettes forming interlaced triangles are ornamental forms of the Star of David or Creator's Star, symbolizing the uniting of the spiritual and physical aspects of God's and man's existence (see pp. 33-34). The circles in the centers of the rosettes with

FIGURE 50

Figure 50: Ceiling detail in Getty Museum

their various divisions, triangles and squares inside are *representing* the Godhead, earthly existence, the Star of Bethlehem, and the Creator's Star. (See pp. 28, 29, 32, and 34 for more details.)

Another common practice was to make elaborate ornamental designs of vines in which the leaves emit an impression of bursting flowers. Flower gardens are associated with Paradise and as such *symbolize* the "Fields of the Blessed, the 'better land,' the abode of souls," while vines are symbolic of life itself (J. C. Cooper, *Traditional Symbols,* p. 70).

When a group of these ornamental designs are situated at the top of columnar posts they are called capitals, and quite a few are on the facade on the ZCMI store front in Salt Lake City, Utah. The building was constructed in 1876 and the facade was added in 1902. A replica of one of the posts with the capital is in the new Museum of Church History and Art in Salt Lake City, Utah.

Figures 51 and 52: ZCMI Store

They are quite similar to those found in the Manti and Salt Lake temples, but with some variations. Just below the cornice, some of the capitals on the storefront have an equilateral triangle in the center, while others have two round circles in the same spot. Each of the cornices has a six-pointed rosette in the middle. Above each capital is a pair of stylized vines with two six-pointed designs at the top, which appear like a cross between a leaf and a blossom. The circles, triangles, and six-pointed rosettes point toward divinity, eternity, and the Holy Trinity, while the six-pointed vine-designs, substituting for the Star of David, are made more alive by the vines nourishing them. (See pp. 28, 32, and 34.)

Several of these ornamental capitals are situated at the top of columns in the J. Paul Getty Museum, some of which have a six-petal rosette

Figure 53: Capital detail in Getty Museum

on each of its four sides with a six-division heart in the center. The great emphasis on them is with the display of flowing vines that seem almost alive. Vines were frequently used in the Bible, Book of Mormon and Jewish writings as a symbol of Jewish and Christian churches and the life of Jesus Christ (see p. 153). Other capitals in the Getty museum include five- and seven-petal rosettes.

The most prolific use of symbols I have discovered is in Aruba, a Dutch island off the coast of Venezuela. Aruba was controlled by the West India Company in the mid 1700's. They brought Indians from Colombia that were good in cement plastering. They began using flower and geometric symbols in cement to decorate houses, churches and other buildings because it was something new and made the buildings more beautiful. By 1900 Dutch settlers were also making the symbols in wood.

Many of the symbols are in vertical columns with from five to eight units consisting of formal flower designs. At least one is geometric, with six points equivalent to a six-pointed star or interlaced triangles, or with eight points and has interlaced squares. Some of them consist of blunt-end crosses—the same as those on the Logan Tabernacle (see figure 45). A general refacing of many buildings was begun about 1975 to salvage the old Dutch style of buildings and their symbols. A new, large mall was constructed with many wide hallways and small shops and stores. Several dozen of the vertical columns, copied from the originals, are

Figure 54: Vertical columns in Aruba

placed along the sides of the hallways. Occasionally there are horizontal rows of circles and rows of squares with an X inside of each. As described in this chapter the circles, squares, crosses, interlaces, triangles and other designs symbolize different aspects of man's lifespan and God's dealings with him, while the X's represent the merging of both the spiritual and physical.

Not so numerous on the buildings are five-pointed stars similar to the ones on the Logan City Tabernacle (see figure 44), and wheel-style symbols with eight or twelve spokes on each. But especially interesting are the Alpha and Omega symbols arched over some of the windows that are almost identical to those on the Salt Lake and Manti temples (see figures 42 and 43), which represent Christ as Alpha and Omega, the Great I AM.

Figure 55: New facing on building in Aruba.

The back of an Etruscan mirror is depicted in *Roman Mythology,* by
Stewart Parowne, on page 51. The Etruscans flourished in central Italy
between 300 and 600 B.C.

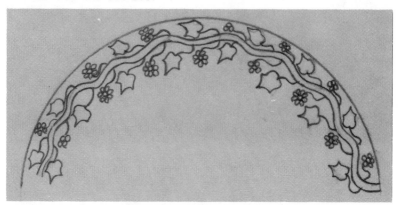

Figure 56: Partial drawing from Etruscan mirror

Around the outer edge of the illustrative drawing on the mirror is a
wreath of vines similar to those on the door knobs and escutcheons on
the Manti Temple doors. The relief on the door knobs is very precise,
with stylized leaves and vines, while the drawing of the Etruscan mirror
is quite rough with plain leaves and stylized flowers. The flowers vary,
with three to eight circles, for petals, on each stem, some of which have
a circle in the center. Vines are symbolic of the lifegiving influence of
the life of Christ while flowers are the same as the rosettes explained
above according to the number of petals on each.

The Gospel of Jesus Christ can be a source of light to guide the life
of whoever wishes to accept it. Attending and understanding the
symbolism, eternal messages and significance of the ordinances of the
temples of The Church of Jesus Christ of Latter-day Saints and the
genealogical services associated with those temples will greatly increase
the spiritual power of the individual, enabling him or her to enter into
exaltation.

BIBLIOGRAPHY

LDS Sources and Abbreviations

Answers | Joseph Fielding Smith, *Answers to Gospel Questions*, Vols. 15, Salt Lake City, Deseret Book Co., 1957.

Archeology | Milton R. Hunter, *Archaeology and the Book of Mormon*, Salt Lake City: Deseret Book Co., 1956.

Bible Dictionary | *LDS Bible Dictionary*, Salt Lake City: The Church of Jesus Christ of Latter-day Saints, 1979.

BYU Fireside | Theodore M. Burton, *Brigham Young Devotional*, Provo Marriott Center, 26 Oct., 1982.

B of M Evidence | Dewey Farnsworth, *Book of Mormon Evidences in Ancient America*, Salt Lake City: Deseret Book Co., 1953.

Christ in America | Milton R. Hunter, *Christ in Ancient America*, Salt Lake City: Deseret Book Co., 1972.

Discourses of Young | Brigham Young, *Discourses of Brigham Young*, by John A. Widstoe, Salt Lake City: Deseret Book Co., 1951.

Discourses of Pratt | Orson Pratt, *Masterful Discourses and Writings of Orson Pratt*, Comp. by N.B. Lundwall, Salt Lake City: Bookcraft, Inc., 1962.

Doctrines of Salv.	Joseph Fielding Smith, *Doctrines of Salvation*, Vols. 1 to 3, Salt Lake City: Bookcraft, Inc., 1956.
Hist. of Church	*Comprehensive History of the Church*, Vol. 7, Salt Lake City: Deseret News Press, 1930.
Gospel Doctrine	Joseph F. Smith, *Gospel Doctrine: Sermons and Writings*, Salt Lake City: Deseret News Press, Early Edition, 1961.
House of Lord	James E. Talmage, *The House of the Lord*, Salt Lake City, Bookcraft, Inc., 1963.
Jesus The Christ	James E. Talmage, *Jesus The Christ*, Salt Lake City: Deseret News Press, 1922.
Journal	*Journal of Discourses* , Vols. 126, Liverpool, 1855-1886
Key To Theology	Parley P. Pratt, *Key to Theology*, Salt Lake City: Deseret Book Co., 1943.
Leadership	Sterling W. Sill, *Leadership*, Salt Lake City: Bookcraft, Inc., 1958.
Life Eternal	Lynn A. McKinlay, *Life Eternal*, Published series of lectures, Bountiful, No publisher, 1949.
Mormon Doctrine	Bruce R. McConkie, *Mormon Doctrine*, Salt Lake City: Bookcraft, Inc., 1958.
M. and Masonry	E. Cecil McGavin, *Mormonism and Masonry*, Salt Lake City: Bookcraft, Inc., 1954.
Origin and Destiny	Joseph Fielding Smith, *Man, His Origin and Destiny*, Salt Lake City: Deseret Book Co., 1954.

Perfection   Joseph Fielding Smith, *The Way to
                        Perfection*, Salt Lake City: Deseret
                        Book Co., 1943.

Power From High   Chapter 12, 1937 Genealogical classes,
                        Power From on High, Salt Lake City:
                        Church Historian's Office.

Priesthood Government   John A. Widstoe, *Priesthood and
                        Church Government*, Salt Lake City:
                        Deseret Book Co., 1966.

Promised Messiah   Bruce R. McConkie, *The Promised
                        Messiah*, Salt Lake City: Deseret Book
                        Co., 1978.

Saviors   Archibald F. Bennett, *Saviors on Mt.
                        Zion,* Deseret Sunday School Manual,
                        Salt Lake City.

Sermons   *Sermons and Missionary Services*, by
                        Bryant S. Hinckley, Salt Lake City:
                        Deseret Book Co., 1949.

Teachings   *Teachings of the Prophet Joseph Smith*,
                        comp. by Joseph Fielding Smith, Salt
                        Lake City: Deseret News Press, 1942.

Temples   N.B. Lundwall, (Compiler), *Temples of
                        The Most High*, Salt Lake City: Zions
                        Printing and Publishing Co., 1945 ed.

Three Degrees   Melvin J. Ballard, *Three Degrees of
                        Glory*, pamphlet of Discourses in Ogden
                        Tabernacle, Salt Lake City: Deseret
                        Book Co., 1922.

Tree of Life   Irme M. Briggs, *Tree of Life Symbolism
                        in Ancient America*, unpublished thesis,
                        Provo: Brigham Young University
                        Library.

U G & H   *Utah Genealogical and Historical Mag.*,
                        Vols. 131, Salt Lake City: Deseret News
                        Press, 1910-1940.

Vision	Joseph Smith, *The Vision*, Compiled by N. B. Lundwall, Salt Lake City: Bookcraft, Inc., N.D.
Vitality	James E. Talmage, *Vitality of Mormonism*, Salt Lake City: Deseret Book Co., 1919..
Word of Wisdom	John A. Widstoe, *The Word of Wisdom*, Salt Lake City: Deseret Book Co., 1938.

LDS Scriptures

Book of Mormon	*Book of Mormon*, Salt Lake City: The Church of Jesus Christ of Latter-day Saints.
D & C	*Doctrine and Covenants*, Salt Lake City: The Church of Jesus Christ of Latter-day Saints.
P of GP	*Pearl of Great Price*, Salt Lake City: The Church of Jesus Christ of Latter-day Saints.
Bible	*The Holy Bible, King James Version*, Salt Lake City: The Church of Jesus Christ of Latter-day Saints.

Non LDS Sources and Abbreviations

Amulets	E.A. Wallis Budge, *Amulets and Talismans*, New Hyde Park: University Books, 1961.
Behold The Sign	Ralph M. Lewis, Imperator of Rosicrucian Order, *Behold The Sign*, San Jose: Rosicrucian Press, LTA, Kingsport, 1944.
Christian Symbols	Frederick Rest, *Our Christian Symbols*, Philadelphia: Christian Education Press, 1954.

Church Symbols	Frederick R. Webber, *Church Symbolism*, Cleveland: J.H. Hansen Pub. 1938 and 1971.
Funk and Wagnall	Funk and Wagnall *Dictionary of Folklore*, San Francisco: Harper and Row, reprint 1984.
Jewish Symbols	Irwin Goodenough, *Jewish Symbols*, New York, Pantheon Books, 1953.
Life Symbols	Elizabeth E. Goldsmith, *Life Symbols as Related to Sex Symbols*, New York: Knickerbocker Press, 1928.
Lost Continent	James Churward, *Lost Continent of Mu*, New York: Ives Washburn, 1933.
Lost Language	Harold Bailey, *Lost Language of Symbolism*, Lakeville Roman, 1912 and 1974.
Migration of Symbols	Count Gobet D'Alviella, *The Migration of the Symbols*, New York: University Books Inc., 1972.
Modern Universe	Raymond A. Littleton, *Modern Universe*, New York: Harper and Brothers, 1956.
Nature of Universe	Fred A. Hoyle, *The Nature of the Universe*, New York: Harper and Brothers, 1950 and 1960.
Pagan and Christian	Thomas Insman, *Ancient Pagan and Modern Christian Symbolism*, New York: Peter Eckler, 1922.
Realm of Nebulae	Edwin L. Hubble, *The Realm of the Nebulae*, New Haven: Yale University Press, Early Edition.
Sacred Symbols	James Churchward, *The Sacred Symbols of Mu*, New York: Ives Washburn, 1933-1960.

Sacred Symbols in Art	Elizabeth E. Goldsmith, *Sacred Symbols in Art*, New York: Knickerbocker Press, 1929.
Signs and Symbols	George Ferguson, *Signs and Symbols in Christian Art*, New York: Oxford University Press, 1966.
Picture Book	Ernest Lehner, *The Picture Book of Symbols*, New York: Um. Penn Publishing Corp, 1956.
Myth and Symbol	R. T. Rundle Clark, *Myth and Symbol in Ancient Egypt,* London, Thames and Hudson, 1978.
Traditional Symbols	J. C. Cooper, *An Illustrated Encyclopedia of Traditional Symbols,* London, Thames and Hudson, 1978.

INDEX OF SYMBOLS AND THEIR COUNTERPARTS

Word Key — **Counterpart**

A

Abodes, differences in earthly — Levels of heavenly mansions—46

Adam and Eve hide from God — People hide from the Lord's representatives—58

Adam, dealings of God with — Dealings of the Lord with man—62

Adam free to choose — Man free to choose—56

Adam suffered consequences — Man will reap consequences of his actions—56

Adam's rib to create Eve — Natural process for creation of man—56

Adopted into Christ's family — Born again through baptism—82

Agency in premortal life — Agency of man—53

Alpha and Omega — All-encompassing nature of Christ—145, 162, 174

Angel Moroni statue — Proclamation of gospel—140

All-seeing eye — Eyes of the Lord—24

All-seeing eye — They looketh from heaven—147

All-searching eye — Leader of the saints—24

Altars, kneeling at — In presence of God and angels—131

Annointing with oil — Officiator represents power of God—90

Aprons, fig leaf — Man's effort to cover up mistakes—58

183

B

Baptism	Death, burial, resurrection—79
Baptism	Godhead—83
Baptism	Atoning blood; birth to life of righteousness—82
Baptism	Born again; birth of a baby; cleansing—81
Baptism by fire	Holy Ghost as if by fire—83
Baptism for the dead	Baptism for the living—111
Baptism of Christ	Jonah swallowed by whale—80
Baptism of Christ and man	Witness of obedience—80
Baptism of earth	Creation; life and death of man—85
Baptism of earth by fire	Earth born again by purifying—116
Baptism of Holy Ghost	Refining and purifying—83
Baptism of Jesus	Baptism of man—80
Baptismal font	Sea in which many are baptized—23, 123
Baptismal font in basement	Similitude of grave for baptisms for the dead—131
Beasts, four	Classes of beings in their destined sphere—54
Beehive	Industry—148
Beehive and deseret	Land of milk and honey—150
Birth into church	Birth of mortal baby—82
Blood on door posts	Obedience of man—64
Blood, spilling on altar	Spilling of Christ's blood—65
Blood of passover and Christ	Giving of one's life and receiving immortal life—65
Bodies, mortal	Spirit bodies—45
Bodies, spiritual	Temporal creation of bodies—54
Bones not broken	Christ's bones not broken—65
Born again by baptism	Adopted into family of Christ—83
Bread and wine	Flesh and blood of Christ—88

Breath entered bones

Bride
Bride, Holy City adorned as
Bridegroom

Spiritual liquid enters immortal
    bodies—121
Church of Jesus Christ—102
Church adorned as a bride—119
The Savior—102

C

Celestial globe
Ceremony, temple
Cherubim
Cherubim, wings of
Christ and church, union of

Christ, bear record of
Christ, church subject to

Christ cast down
Christ, hunger of
Christ, first born
Christ lifted onto cross

Christ loved church
Christ's perfect life
Christmas
Church of Jesus Christ
Circle

Circle and square, combined

Circles on temple doors

City of Zion

Clothing, white
Cloud

Sea of glass and fire—123
Plan of salvation—130
Angels and guardians—137
Power to act—137
Marriage of husband and
    wife—119
All things—54
Wives subject to their
    husbands—102
Man yields to temptation—16
Hunger of man for gospel—15
Firstling of flock—64
Man lifted up by the
    Father—68
Husbands love wives—102
Lamb without blemish—65
Birth of Jesus—17
The bride—102
Perfection; divinity; endless
    universe: eternal life—28, 165, 168
Progression from earthly
    imperfection towards
    perfection—30, 145
Eternity; everlasting life;
    etc.—149, 167
Twelve symbolic divisions
    of—22
Purity of thought—138
Lord's guiding hand; power of
    presence—19

Clouds, embossed   Gospel dispelling clouds of
                            error—147

Clouds of heaven   Sign of Son of Man—20
Coats of skins   High moral standards—138
Coats of skins   Robes of righteousness; proper
                            clothing—60,138

Commandments, Adam and   Mankind breaking
  Eve breaking   commandments—73
Compass, sign of   Boundary of passion—35, 36
Consecration, law of   Equality in government of
                            God—96

Cornerstone, Christ as   All things pointing to Christ
                            and atonement—66

Cornerstones, four of temple   Christ; revelation; Book of
                            Mormon, and restoration—129

Covenants, temple   Laws and covenants of earth
                            and heaven—134

Creation, spiritual   Temporal creation—55
Crook in staff   Understanding heart—97
Cross, Christ lifted onto   Moses lifted up brazen
                            serpent—67

Cross, crucifixion   Christ on the cross—27
Cross, equal arms   Four corners and powers of
                            heaven and earth—28

Cross, T   Hammer and avenger—27
Cup, the   Christ's agony and
                            obedience—88

Curtains, drawing back   Admitting souls to
                            paradise—137

D

Deseret   Honey bee—150
Doors, stylized   Access to temple and the
                            gospel—154

Dove, offering of dove   Purification of the woman—85
Dove, sign of   Holy Ghost descending—84
Dress, uniform   All men equal—138

E

Earth, as Urim and Thummin	Urim and Thummim sets—123
Earth, baptism of Holy Ghost	Cleansing of earth by fire—86
Earth, death of	Death of many martyres—118
Earth's baptism of Holy Ghost	Earth shall burn as an oven—116
Endowment, temple	Course of instruction and endowment of power—133
Eternal knowledge	Education on earth—94
Eve	Mother of all women—57
Eye, Allseeing	Divine protection; omniscience of the father—24
Eyes, Eve's opened	Man learns good from evil—61
Excuses of Adam and Eve	Excuses of mankind—59
Experiences, purpose of in heaven	Purpose of experiences in mortal life—53

F

Faith to control a universe	Faith to accomplish things on earth—78
Family in heaven	Family on earth—49
Family life in heaven	Family life on earth—100
Fall of Adam	Fall of man—62
Firstling of flock	First born, Jesus Christ—64
Father and mother in heaven	Father and mother on earth—45
Fig leaf aprons	Man's effort to cover up mistakes—58
Fire, pillar of	Bright light—20
Fire	Method of destruction—117
Flame on finials	Light of the gospel—141
Flesh and bones	Immortality—121
Flesh and blood	Mortality—121
Flesh covered bones	Method of resurrection—121
Flood of earth	Washed away sins of earth—85
Footstool, Lord's	Earth—21

Free agency of Adam — Free agency of man—56

Fruit of tree — Mortal law—56

G

Gash in Christ's side — Atonement has been wrought—68

Gateway to Kingdom of Heaven — Baptism into Kingdom of God—79

Garments — Moral cleanliness and priesthood power—138

Gate to Celestial Kingdom — Circling flames of fire—120

Glory of God — Glory of the sun—123

Glory, three degrees of — Sun; moon; stars—46

God as father of Jesus Christ — Abraham as father of nations—65

God's perfection — Ten commandments—91

Gold, frankincense and myrrh — Purity and divinity—18

Government of God, equality in — Earthly law of consecration—96

Grave, borrowed — Descended below all things—18

Ground cursed for Adam's sake — Struggle of mankind—60

H

Hands, clasped — Brotherly love and fellowship—146

Hands, laying of by God — Man laying hands on for ordinances—84

Hand, left — Perverse—20

Hand of Lord, right — Power and authority—20

Hand, right — Righteousness—20

Hand, uplifted — Covenant with God—136

Heavenly parents, relationship — Temple marriage or sealing—101

Heavenly things — All things earthly—53

Hell — State of wicked in spirit world—106

Holiness to the Lord — Dedication toward temple covenants—126

Holy City — Twelve symbolic divisions of—22

Holy City — Lambs wife—119
Holy City as a bride — Church adorned as a bride—119
Holy City, celestialized — Glory of God; light of, etc.—119

House of the Lord, the — The Lord's dwelling place—126

I

Interwoven letters on temple door — The house of the Lord—153
Isaac, obedient offering of — Obedience of mankind's service—65

J

Jasper, pure gold, crystal, etc., — Symbol of Holy City—120
Jonah, sign of — Warning to all mankind—80
Jonah swallowed by whale — Baptism of man—80
Joy in celestial glory — Joy on earth—50
Joy of creating eternally — Joys of family life—73

L

Lake of fire and brimstone — Torment of wicked in spirit world—106

Lamb without blemish — Christ's perfect life—65
Lamb's wife — Holy City of celestialized earth—119

Lamps of virgins — Church membership—94
Life in heaven — Life on earth—50
Line, straight — Absolute truth—37
Loin cloth — Christ's clothing at death—27
Lord, the — The bridegroom—94
Lord's prayer — Communication on earth and in heaven—97

M

Manger	Lowest of all things—17
Manna falling from heaven	Partaking of the sacrament—88
Mansions, levels of	Differences in earthly abodes—46
Menorah, Jewish	Tree; law; tree of life—38
Mediator, Christ as	Man as a mediator—77
Moon	Terrestrial glory—47
Mortality, experiences in	Instruction and experiences in premortality—46

N

Noah's ark	Not another flood—116

O

Obedience of Isaac and Christ	Obedience of mankind—65
Offerings, burnt, sin, and peace	Smoke ascending to heaven, the people, and peace with God—66
Olive branch wreathes	Branches of Israelites—153
Olive oil, pure	Emblem of purity for ordinances—90
Ordinances, temple	Ordinances of earth and heaven—134
Organize, God's pattern	Organize according to flesh—74
Organization of universe	Organization of church—77

P

Paradise	State of righteous in spirit world—106
Parents, eternal teach spirit children	Parents teach children—103
Passover, blood on door post	Destroyer will pass by obedient—64
Patriarchal order in heaven	Temple marriage or sealing—99

Pinnacle — High place or situation—16
Plan of salvation — Temple ceremony—130
Priesthood — Governing power of universe—43
Priesthood in heaven — Priesthood on earth—74
Pyramid, double — Union of fire and water, baptism—36

Q

Quetzacoatl — Christ and devil, in Americas—17
Quetzal bird — Christ's visit to Americas—17
Quetzal Bird, green — Christ as life of world—17

R

Rainbow — Remembrance of the Lord's covenant and glory—116
Rationalization of Eve — Man's rationalization about temptation—58
Refiners fire — Presence of Christ—117
Rebellion of Satan — Rebellion of mankind—53
Remnant of Joseph's coat — Seed to be preserved—19
Room, Celestial — Highest degree of glory—136
Room, Garden — Garden of Eden—136
Room, Terrestrial — Second degree of glory—136
Room, World — Dreary world—136
Rosettes, 4 and 8 pointed — Squares and interlaced squares—154, 165
Rosette, three petal — Stylized triangle—40

S

Sacrament — Sacrifice; baptism; and the Lord's atonement—87
Sacrament, partaking of — Placing blood on door posts; accepting Christ—89
Sacrifice, atoning — Service in church positions—70
Sacrifice, correct — Man's proper attitude toward Christ—64

Sacrifice, obedience of Christ's — Obedience of man's service; obedient offering of Isaac—66

Sacrifices, offering of — Sacrifice of Jesus Christ—64

Salvation, plan of — God's plan for redeeming mankind—71

Sandalls, taking off — Shaking off world—137

Satan, in spirit world — Power of Satan on earth—107

Satan's premortal influence — Satan's mortal influence—53

Savior, the — The bridegroom—102

Savior, Christ a — Church members as saviors on Mount Zion—112

Saviors on Mount Zion — Members doing Genealogical work—112

Scroll on temple doors — Folding and unfolding curtains of heaven—153

Sea of glass and fire — Celestial globe—123

Sealing of Holy Ghost — Sealings in the temples—103

Sealings, proxy — Sealings on behalf of others—113

Serpent — Devil—57

Serpent, cast out — Man cast out from presence of God—68

Serpent in scripture — Christ and devil in America—17

Serpent, faith to look at — Faith of man to accept gospel—67

Serpent, look upon and live — Those who look to Christ may live—67

Serpent or viper — Evil or treacherous person—67

Serpent, Moses lifted up brazen — Christ lifted onto cross—67

Serpent of brass — Christ on cross—17

Service of Jesus Christ — Man's service in the church—97

Seven, number of — Seven beasts, years, days, seals, trumpets, etc.—37, 168

Sheep — Church members and others—97

Shells, scallop-type — New and divine life—154

Shepherd
Shepherd's staff — Watcher over mankind—18
Church office and authority—97

Shepherds — Members in church positions—97

Son of man, sign of — Clouds of heaven—20
Spires and 12 pinnacles — First Presidency, apostles, etc.—141

Spires on the east — Church on eastern hemisphere—141

Spires on the west — Church on western hemisphere—141

Spirit bodies — Mortal bodies—45
Spirit world, deeds in — Judgment for deeds on earth—110

Spirit world, teaching gospel in — Teaching gospel on earth—109
Spirit world, repentance in — Repentance on earth—111
Spirits in prison — Intermediate state in spirit world—108

Square — Earth's existence; four corners of earth—29

Square and circle combined — Man's efforts to be perfect—30,145

Square over rosette — Interlaced squares—39, 40
Square, sign of — Justice; uprightness; morality—36

Star — Divine guidance—18, 164
Star, eight pointed — Eight principles and roads to heaven—30

Star, five pointed — Star of Bethlehem; divine guidance—31, 164

Star on Assembly Hall — Creators star; interlaced triangles—39

Star, six points — Six days of week and of creation—34

Stars — Telestial glory—47
Stars fall from heaven — Members falling away from church—118

Stone | Gospel or Kingdom of God—16
Stone, white | Urim and Thummin for inhabitants—123
Stones, earth | Gospel for the whole earth—142
Stones, earth | Life on earth and telestial glory—143
Stones, moon | Terrestrial glory—143
Stones, points on sun | Rays of light—143
Stones, Saturn | Possibly Kolob—144
Stones, sun | Celestial glory—143
Stubble | Wicked that are easily blown—117
Subtlety of Satan with Eve | Man's rationalization about temptation—58
Sun | The circle—29
Sun | Celestial glory—47
Sun darkened | Apostate darkness—118
Sun, moon, stars | Three degrees of glory—46
Sustain God and Christ | Sustain leaders of the church—76
Swaddling clothes | Restrictions of life—18
Sword, Flaming | Authority of God—137

T

Talents, parable of | Service in the church—94
Taps, three | Act of pennance—137
Temple, four cornerstones of | Christ; revelation; Book of Mormon; and restoration—129
Temple, man as a | May become a temple of righteousness—160
Temple marriage or sealing | Heavenly parents, relationship—101
Temple structure | Architectural work above—114
Temples, holy | Heavenly Kingdom of God—160
Telestial glory | Earth in mortal state—115
Terrestrial glory | Earth in millennial state—115

Tithing, for celestial kingdom

Tree of knowledge

Tree of life
Triangles, abbreviation of
  interlaced
Triangles, combining of

Triangles, combined

Triangle, equilateral

Triangles, interlaced

Triangles, union of

Triangles, up and down

Twelve in City of Zion

Twelve in Holy City

Twelve oxen

Tithing, necessary for
  temple—96
Mankind's attainments on
  earth—60
Love of God—37
X—36

Uniting of spiritual and
  material planes of life—34
Father and mother in
  heaven—33
United purpose and attributes
  of Godhood; water spirit and
  blood, etc.—31, 32
Star of David; Creator's
  star—34
Union of male and female
  creators—33
Directions of thoughts between
  God and man—32
Twelve temples; thrones;
  apostles, etc.—23
Gates; foundations; oxen,
  etc.—22
Twelve gates; twelve tribes—24

U

Uncircumsized prohibited
  passover
Universe, Eternal Father
  does in
Urim and Thummin

Non-members not to partake
  of the sacrament—89
All one does in
  righteousness—74
Means of revelation—35

V

Valley of dry bones
Veil of temple

People in their graves—121
Figurative curtain—137

Virgins, parable of — Preparation for Kingdom of Heaven—119

Virgins, ten — Kingdom of heaven—119

W

Washing — Purification—137

Wedding, entrance to — Entrance to celestial kingdom—119

Wedding Ring — Marriage union; lasting love; eternity—11

Wilderness — Gentile nations; world—15

Word of Wisdom — Purity one must attain—95

Worship of devil — Worship of power and material—16

Wreath of vines — Spiritual life of Jesus Christ—153

X

X, abbreviation of — Straight line—37

X, Geometrical — Abbreviation of interlaced triangles—36, 168

TOPICAL INDEX

A

Abraham, to offer son—65
Abbreviation, of symbols—35, 166
Abodes—143
Adam, as head of
  household—56
Adam, created from dust—56
Adam, fall of—63
Adam and Eve, began to
  labor—63
Adam and Eve, cast out—61
Adam and Eve, chastized—59
Adopted, into family of
  Christ—83
Adoption, whereby we cry
  Abba—83
Agency, free, regard to
  consequences—72
Agency, the right to choose—53
All seeing eye—24, 147
Alpha and Omega—145, 162, 174
Altar, at, eternal love—131
Androgyne, nature—33
Angels, in heaven—101
Annointing, the sick—90
Apostasy, shall cover the
  earth—118
Aprons, fig leaf—58
Ark—84, 116, 137
Atonement—63, 64, 65
Atonement, consists of a
  process—69
Atonement, priest shall
  make—85

Atonement, sacrament points
  toward—87
Attitude, death will not
  change—107
Authority, in proper way—77
Authority, sustaining of—76

B

Babel, tower of—150
Baptism, as Jonah was
  swallowed—80
Baptism, gateway into God's
  kingdom—79
Baptism, method of—79
Baptism, of the Holy Ghost—83
Baptism, the only valid—86
Beasts, four—54
Beehive—150
Big dipper—stars, 147
Bind, on earth—113
Blemish, without spot or—82
Blessings, conditioned upon
  temple service—157
Blood, on doors—89
Blood, replaced with spiritual
  fluid—121
Blood, spilled upon the
  altar—65
Blossom, in form of star—153
Body, shall be restored—120
Body, spirit, shapes growing
  body—54
Body, raised to immortal—121
Bodies, celestial, terrestrial,
  telestial—47

Bodies, resurrected—121
Bodies, spirit, grew in
  stature—52
Bones, came together—121
Bones, not to be broken—65
Borrowed grave, buried—18
Bow, in the cloud—116
Bread of life—16
Breath, entered the bones—121
Bride—102
Bride, Lamb's wife—119
Bridegroom—94, 102, 119
Brimstone, and fire—106
Burial, baptized after manner
  of—82
Buttresses—141

C

Candlestick—38
Ceremony, temple—130
Chain, that binds—112
Cherubim—60, 61, 137
Child, earth like newborn—85,
  86
Child, newborn—81
Children, spirit—46, 52, 53, 62,
  91
Children, to their parents—132
Christ, foreordained—63
Christ, lifted up on cross—68
Christ, in ancient America—141
Christ, on the cross—27
Christ, attributes of—68
Christ, preached unto the
  spirits—108
Christ, spirit child—44
Christ, the mediator—77
Christ, the sign of—20
Christ, to reign on earth—115
Christ, subdued enemies—63,
  106

Christ, to come in power—118
Christ, turned from inn—17
Christ, was obedient—66
Christmas, commemorate birth
  of Jesus—17
Church, of Jesus Christ—26
Church, organization of—77
Church position, called into—76
Circle, never ending
  existence—29, 165, 168, 174, 176
Circle, symbol of universe—29, 165
Circle, with rays—147
Circles, on temple doors—152, 167
City of Zion—23
Claim, to gospel symbols—26
Clasped hands—146
Clothing, all alike in white—138
Cloud, representative of His
  glory, power and presence—19
Clouds, embossed—147
Coat, of many colors—18
Coats, of skins—60, 138
Commandments—56, 58, 90,
  104, 110
Commandments, "Thou shalt
  not"—91
Compass, boundary of
  passion—36
Consecration, law of—96
Consequences—16, 73
Cornerstones, in temples—128
Cornerstone, of Zion—141
Cornerstone, of gospel—66
Covenant, born in—132
Covenant, never again flood—116
Covenants, temple—134
Created—54, 55
Creation—42, 44
Creator, life flowing from—32
Creator, male, female—33
Cross, equal arms—28, 164, 169, 174

Cross, four beasts—28
Cross, most common—27
Cross, crucifixation—27
Crucifixion, cross—27
Cup—87
Curtain, veil—147
Curtain, of heaven—137, 153

D

Dead, baptism for—111, 131, 137
Dead, Proxy for—131
Dead, I saw hosts of—109
Deseret—150
Designs, many and vary—37
Devil, taken captive by—106
Divine, perfection of the Father
  and Son—30
Domain, His posterity—49
Dominions—99, 125
Doors, entrance into
  church—155
Doors, on temple—148
Dove, bodily shape like a—84
Dove, emblem of purity—85
Drink, strong—95

E

Earth, baptism of—85, 116
Earth, became corrupted—86
Earth, creation of—55
Earth, four quarters of—142
Earth, form of a cross—28
Earth, is mortal—144
Earth, lifespan—85, 115
Earth, to people the—95
Earth, prepared for celestial
  glory—118
Earth, whereon these may
  dwell—52
Earthly, conforming to
  heavenly—41

Earthstones—142, 147
Education—94
Eight-pointed star, man's
  regeneration—30, 168
Elements, of the earth—116
Elijah, mission of—112
Endowment, four distinct
  parts—135
Endowment, involves two
  qualities—133
Endowment, is protection—156
Endowment, to receive all—132
Estate, first and second—71
Eve—61, 102
Eve, first mother—57
Eye, inside circle—147
Eyes of the Lord—24
Exaltation, both have
  attained—124
Exaltation, continuation of
  seeds—101
Exaltation, singly without—101
Existence, ante-mortal—63
Experience, chain of
  authority—77
Experience, how to
  distinguish—74

F

Face, shall be unveiled—153
Faith, first step on ladder—78
Faith, to be healed—67
Faith, to construct and people a
  world—78
Family, as eternal unit—124
Family, groups, celestial—49
Family, father head of his—99, 102
Family, is a kingdom—99
Family, man have his own—49
Family, will have fullness of
  joy—50

Fashion, opinions of—139
Father and Mother in
  heaven—33
Father, creations of—53
Father, omniscience of—24
Fig, tree—118
Finial, a sculptured flame—141
Fire, and brimstone—106
Fire, by the Lord—117
Fire, to purity—83
Five pointed stars on
  Temple—31
Flaming fire, at Kirtland
  temple—19
Flaming sword—137
Flesh, came up—121
Flock, firstlings of the—64
Flowers, in same cluster—33
Font, baptismal, in
  basement—131
Footstool—21
Foundation, of the apostles—129
Four corners—29
Four, great powers—28
Free, to choose—56
Freedom, complete—73

G

Galaxies, part of larger
  systems—42
Garden of Eden—56, 57, 60,
  102, 135, 137
Garments, as a protection—138
Garments, of holy
  priesthood—139
Garments, washed—82
Gate, heirs will enter—120
Genealogical, work—157
Globe, celestialized—115
Globe, will be Urim and
  Thummin—123

Glories, celestial, terrestrial,
  telestial—143
Glory, celestial—50, 77, 100,
  103, 123, 147
Glory, degrees of—46
God, angels of—101
God, communion with—155
God, once as we are—48
God, the Father has a wife—33
God, what makes—49
Gods, learn how to be—48
Godhead, nature of—44
Godhood—49, 111, 168
Good and evil, experience—61
Gospel, preached unto all—110
Gospel, spiritual realms—138
Gospel, to help us develop—133
Governs, all things—43
Grave, beyond the—105
Graves, I have opened—121
Ground, cursed—60

H

Hand, symbol—20
Hand, guiding in form of
  cloud—19
Hand, right—21, 76, 146
Hands, laying on of—116
Hands, vote with uplifted—136
Heart, pure in—155
Hearts, desire of their—110
Hearts, of the fathers—112
Heaven, paradise of God—54
Heaven, with lands, houses—51
Heaven, new—119
Heavens, can be no
  confusion—77
Heavens, multiply—42
Heirship, capable of—72
Hell, is spirit prison—107
Hell, the word—106

Hinges, on temple doors—153
Holy city, adorned as a
  bride—119
Holy Ghost, as an oven—116
Holy Ghost, baptism of—84
Holy Ghost, is a personage—84
Holy spirit, of promise—100,
  103, 114
Holy of Holies—139, 169
Honey bee—150
House of the Lord—126, 153,
  155
House, where he could
  reveal—133
Husband and wife, in post-
  mortal life—101
Husbands, love your wives—102

I

Ideas, man-made, have become
  corrupted—15
Immortality—122
Industry—152
Influence, Satan's—59, 62
Inherit, all heights and
  depths—48
Inherit, through all eternity—100,
  101
Inheritance, with the Father—124
Instruction, course of—135
Interlaced triangle or six-pointed
  star—34
Isaac, the only begotten son—65
Israelites, take the blood from
  lambs—64

J

Jesus, depicted clothed—27
Jonah, was immersed—80
Joy—50
Joy, fullness of—73

Judged by the Lord—122
Judged, in this life, and spirit
  world—110

K

Key word—123
Kindgom, celestial—120, 127
Kingdom, celestial, cut off
  from—90
Kingdom, celestial, cannot
  abide—122
Kingdom, in the Father's—46
Kingdom, of activity—50
Kingdom, of God, birth
  into—82
Knowledge—95, 124, 133
Knowledge, died without—110
Kolob—144

L

"L", is sign of builder,
  uprightness—36, 166
"L", or sign of square—35
L, the letter—152, 166
Lamb, without blemish—65
Lamb, for burnt offering—85
Land, flowing with honey—150
Lamps, of foolish virgins—94
Lamps, oil in—119
Lamps, source of light—155
Law, pointing to sacrifice—66
Life, eternal—48, 69, 153, 161
Life, eternal, continuation of the
  seeds—124
Life, family, to teach—100
Life, mortal is the time—110
Life, post-mortal, to create—73
Life, premortal—72, 73
Light, that groweth brighter—124
Lord, appointed
  messengers—109

Lord, submitted to being
baptized—80
Love, between husband and
wife—100
Love, feelings of—102
Lucifer, will have no
influence—108

M

Man, become mortal—61
Man, may be restored—69
Man, must sacrifice all
things—66
Man, origin of—45, 55
Mankind, experiences those
things—46
Mankind, nature of—44
Manger, of Jesus—18
Marrriage, covenant—101
Marriage, of Christ and the
Church—119
Marriage, to keep intact—158
Marriage, relationship—56, 102
Marriage, temple—130, 131
Marriage, with,
responsibilities—103
Men, judge all—110
Menorah—38
Millennium—115, 118, 120, 123
Mind, belongs to the spirit—105
Mind, tortures of hell—106
Molten, or brazen sea—23
Moon stones—143
Moon, turned to blood—118
Mortality, born into—82
Mothers, teach children—102

N

Name, new written—123
New Jerusalem, built upon the
remnant—19

O

Offering, sin and peace—66
Officiator, performs—103
Offspring—74
Offspring, nature of—125
Oil, for anointing—90
Oil, for the menorah—38
Olive, branch—153
Olive, leaf—154
Olive, tree—90, 154
Ordinance, for exaltation—132
Ordinance, sealing—131
Ordinances, earthly—104
Ordinances, performance of—110
Ordinances, temple—114, 129
Ordinances, to teach and
train—134
Ordinances, washings,
anointings—137
Ordinations, cannot be
performed by spirits—111
Organize, according to men—74
Organization, in spirit
world—109

P

Paradise—108, 137
Paradisiacal, glory—115
Parents, children born to—132
Parents, sealing of children—103
Parents, eternal—52
Passover, feast of the—89
Passover, Lord's—65
Patriarchal, order of the
family—99
Pedigree, ancestral—113
People, try to hide—58
Pedestals—141
Perdition, sons of—122
Perfect, fathers cannot be
made—112

Perfection, attempting to
reach—77, 124, 145
Place, with my loved ones—50
Plan, of Father, not
frustrated—61
Plan of salvation—13, 52, 62,
71, 89, 140
Plan, of salvation,
endowment—133
Plan of salvation, temple—130
Posterity—125
Power, creative—73
Power, from on high—133
Power, healing—90
Power, organize—74
Prayer, a bonding link—97
Prayers, answered in
temple—156
Prepare—60
Priesthood, brings worlds into
existence—44
Priesthood, patriarchal—99
Priesthood, on earth and
heaven—75
Priesthood, organization—75
Priesthood, power—43, 74, 113
Priesthood, quorums—76
Priesthood, signs and
tokens—132
Prison, farthing is paid—107
Prison, house, to come out
of—111
Prison, spirit to be taught
in—108
Problems, that vex life—156
Probation, mortal—122
Progression, man's—144
Prove, see if they will do—71, 72
Proxy, for a bride—112
Proxy, someone acts as—111,
132, 134

Q

Queen, and priestess to her
husband—33
Queen, mother of her increasing
offspring—34
Quorum, when a man dies—109

R

Rainbow—116
Rays, of light—143
Rationalization, steps of—58
Rebirth, of body, mind, and
spirit—32, 168
Rebirth of pre-mortal spirit—81
Records, of offspring—114
Records, genealogical—113
Records, vast system—76
Rehabilitation, means of—107
Remnant, of Joseph was
preserved—19
Remorse, loss of
opportunities—48, 123
Repent, wicked will have to—111
Repentance, strength from—78
Research, genealogical—113
Resurrection—120, 122, 124
Revelation, rock of—129
Revelation, temples a place of—155
Room, sealing—132
Room, world, terrestrial,
celestial—136
Rosette—40, 154, 165, 168, 170, 173, 176

S

Sabbath, on the first day—91
Sacrifice, of Savior—65
Sacrifice, burnt—66
Sacrifice, pointed to Christ—65
Sacrifices, prescribed in set
manner—64

Sacrament, not to partake of—90
Sacrament, to renew
  covenants—87
Sacraments—91
Sanctuaries, for sacred
  rites—126
Sanctuaries, of Satan—128
Satan, Adam refused to
  accept—57
Satan, combat influence—158
Satan, in the spirit world—107
Satan, Lord's encounter with—15
Satan, not given up—62
Satan, power and captivity
  of—73
Satan, tempting Eve—57
Satan, teachings of—103
Satan, the devil—62
Satan, twists truth—67
Saturn stone—144
Saviors, on Mount Zion—112
Savior, accepted God's plan—53
Sealed, as a family—132
Sealed by—103
Sealing, by Holy Spirit—100
Sealing, of husbands and
  wives—113
Sealing, words of—131
Seals—38
Scroll, is unfolded—153
Serpent, beguiled me—59
Serpent, Moses lifted up
  the—67
Serpent, of brass—66
Serpent, symbol of Christ—17
Serpent, the devil—57
Serpent, treacherous—67
Serpent, was subtle—57
Serpents, fiery—66
Servants, ministering—101
Service, temple—134

Service, giving experience—76
Seven-branch, tree—38
Seven, combines square and
  triangle—37
Seven, days, times, years,
  ears—37, 168
Shells, scallop-type—154
Shepherds, at birth of Christ—18
Shepherd's, staff—97
Shepherds, labor with sheep—97
Sign, the Prophet Jonas—80
Signs, and wonders—118
Sin, upon heads of parents—103
Six days—55, 91, 166
Six, points, six days—34
Son of Man, sign of in
  heaven—20
Son of Man, on the right of
  power—20
Solomon's temple—128
Sorrow—60
Spirals, equivalent of a
  circle—29
Spires, or towers—141
Spirit body, form or shape—45
Spirit, contains pure
  elements—122
Spirit, leaves mortal body—105
Spirit, matter—125
Spirit, state—105
Spirit world—105
Spirits, afflicted by evil—107
Spirits, disobedient—108
Spirits, ministering—101
Spiritual death—81, 82
Square, and interlaced
  triangles—35, 168
Square, and compass—145
Square, inferior to circle—29
Squares, interlaced—154, 165, 169, 174
Squares, rows of—145

Star, bright and morning—31
Star, of David—138, 164, 173
Star, of David, on Assembly
  Hall—26, 39, 164, 170
Star, of the East—31, 164
Stars, fall from heaven—118
Stars, five pointed—143, 164, 174
Stars, on temple—144, 169
Stars, twelve pointed—149
State, of righteous—108
State, of spirits,
  intermediate—108
State, mortal—115
State, paradisiacal—117
State, of happiness or
  misery—122
State, in spirit world—106
Statue, of angel Moroni—140
Stone, Gospel of Jesus
  Christ—16
Stubble, easily blown—117
Sun, as a symbol—29
Sun, no need of—120
Sun, shall be darkened—118
Sun, stones—143
Swaddling clothes—17
Sword, flaming—61
Symbols, communication—12
Symbols, meaning of—131

T

Talents, parable of—119
Talents, develop own—94
Tea, and coffee—95
Teachings to the ancient
  prophets—12
Teeth, gnashing of—123
Temple, filled with angels—20
Temple, individual
  testimony—158
Temples, of the Lord—126, 160

Temple, place for all—157
Temple, plans—141
Temple, of revelation—155
Temple, symbolic beacon—126
Temple, unfailing guide—130,
  148
Temptation, Jesus by Satan—15,
  16
Testimony, of genealogical
  activity—159
Tithing, a requirement—96
Tobacco—95
Towers, priesthood—147
Tree, fruit of—57, 58
Tree, of knowledge—56, 60, 67,
  73
Tree, of life—37, 60, 67
Triangle, equilateral—31, 170, 173
Triangle, father, mother and
  child—32
Triangle, of each panel—152
Triangles, interlaced—34, 170, 174
Triangles, position of—32, 36
Twelve, gates, apostles,
  tribes—23, 120, 166
Twelve, on temple—22
Twelve, pinnacles, finials,
  etc.—141

U

Unclean, tabernacle—161
Union, of spiritual with
  material—34
United Order, to establish
  equality—96
Universe—78, 91, 94, 165
Universe, keys of—77
Universe, perfection in—34
Universe, plan of salvation
  in—12
Universe, planets of—145

Universe, power and
  jurisdiction—41
Universe, priesthood
  organization—113
Universe, purpose—46
Universe, scale model—148
Uppermost—33
Urim and Thummim—35, 123

V

"V", or sign of compass—36
Valid, in heaven—104
Valley, of dry bones—121
Veil, drawn between—105
Veil, of the temple—138
Veil, side of—110
Vines, wreath of—153, 169, 173, 176
Virgins, foolish—119
Virgins, lamps of the wise—90
Virgins, parable of—94
Voice, of Lord—58
Vows, perform—136

W

War, in heaven—53
Washings, anointings—137
Wedding—94
Welfare system, teaches
  stewardship—96
White bearded God—16
White stone—123
Wicked, memories—107
Wife, not a servant—102
Wise men, gifts to Jesus—18
Word of Wisdom, to gain
  admittance—95
World, lone and dreary—135
Worship, of power—16
World, sons go and
  organize—50

World, spirit—107, 111
World, telestial—116
World, to govern—90
Worthiness—104
Wreath, olive branch—153

X

"X", merging of physical and
  spiritual—36, 168